MW01593730

Dear Cindy and Martin,

"No man can reveal to you aught but that which already lies half asleep in the dawning of your knowledge."

Kahlil Gibran

Thanks for opening up my heart to what was there

All the best
Paul

Living a *Successful* Life

HOW TO SET
AND ACHIEVE
MEANINGFUL
GOALS

Paul Davis Tillman

INKWATER
PRESS

PORTLAND • OREGON

Copyright 2005 by Paul Davis Tillman
2ndEdition

Interior and cover designed by Masha Shubin

All rights reserved. No part of this book may be reproduced or transmitted in any form or by any means whatsoever, including photo-
copying, recording or by any information storage and retrieval system, without written permission from the publisher. Contact Inkwater Press at 6750 SW Franklin Street, Suite A, Portland, OR 97223.

www.inkwaterpress.com

ISBN 1-59299-160-2

Publisher: Inkwater Press

Printed in the U.S.A.

Table of Contents

"Truth is what stands
the test of experience"

Albert Einstein
Out of My Later Years

Introduction

I believe the purpose of education at all levels; home, church, school, or university should be to teach people how to live a successful life. Any person, if they are truly educated, must be able to function independently, or in cooperation with others, to achieve their goals. They should be able to identify and accomplish goals that enhance their self-esteem and increases their enjoyment of life. Truly meaningful goals should be, either directly or indirectly, a benefit to society. In order to accomplish these ends, a person must know, and be able to use, the full capacity of their human potential.

Teaching people the scope of their human potential must be society's first priority. Because it is from the knowledge and use of their full human potential that harmony, prosperity, sound health and achievement flow. People who know and use their innate powers are an asset to society; they move themselves forward with confidence and achieve great things.

Contained within the scope of our human potential lies the process of goal setting and goal achievement. Learning and using the goal achievement process leads directly to living a successful life as each member of society conceives it to be. Setting and achieving personally meaningful goals not only benefits the person but it indirectly improves the conditions and circumstances of every other member of society. In addition, learning the process of goal setting and achievement unveils the concept of universal law.

Universal law forms the foundation of all beneficial achievement and provides the basis of true personal contentment. When a person understands the nature and scope of these two fundamental laws, and acts in accordance with them, their life becomes more successful and enjoyable in all areas. Conversely, failure to live in accordance with universal law, either knowingly or unknowingly, can cause great harm.

Unfortunately, the process for goal definition and achievement is not taught to the general public. This is because the goals of education are in some areas too narrowly focused. Our leadership; parents, church leaders and educators, do not step back from their immediate concerns and see that a process of goal achievement exists as a complete body of teachable knowledge. We understand the requirement for having goals but we fail to teach how goals are identified and accomplished. Instead society accepts the bits and pieces of the creative process as revealed in nursery rhymes, religion, movies and television and do not ask why they might be true. We do not know why, for example what happens "When you wish upon a star," practice the golden rule, believe in ESP, prayer or miracles. All these things are readily available to us all, but we are not taught why.

The great tragedy, the great injustice and the great failing of our society is that we do not reveal our full human potential by teaching the creative goal achievement process in the general course of education. We dance around the issues and our citizens fail to appreciate their true capabilities. Our failure to teach them their full potential denies them their birthright and the full, successful life they were intended to have.

I am the son of a psychic mother. As I grew up, I saw numerous events on an on going basis that defied a logical explanation but were nonetheless true. They were so much a part of my early life that I accepted them as being part of the natural order. I assumed there must be two methods of explaining life's events; those that could be explained by science and logic and those that could be explained by empirical experiences. I made no judgments about the two aspects of my experience; they were simply part of my world and both equally real to me. This aspect of my life lead me to be open to a new and critical development in my later life.

In Atlanta, Georgia in the mid 1970s, two seemingly ordinary people, Martel and Cindy Day, taught a course called "Progressions." They were, it turns out, anything but ordinary. They had been taught the process of creativity by another teacher, but rather than keeping it to themselves, decided to marshal their strength of character, courage and energy and be of service to their community by teaching it to others.

Their task wasn't easy, especially in my case. Through a series of lectures, the Days made their students aware of the power that each of them contains. They worked from a place that was based on a sincere desire to be of service to humanity. The course saved me from myself and gave me the tools to live a happy and successful life on my own terms. I am deeply grateful for their efforts.

The essence of their course was a process of meditative, self-analysis that tapped into the realm of human creativity. The goal of the course was to reveal a process that would enable the achievement of personally meaningful goals. The process they taught was highly effective and worked for me without fail. I was so intrigued by the dynamics of the class that I became a volunteer and worked with them closely for two years.

Having lived the principles I learned in the "Progressions" class for over 25 years, I knew for certain that having a worthy goal and striving to achieve it forms the foundation of a successful life. I learned that the application of universal laws and the process of creativity provided a dramatic, lasting improvement in every aspect of my life. In "Progressions" I was taught many other lessons and skills which are also presented here as they too have served me well.

After leaving "Progressions," I continued my study of human potential on my own. I was not surprised to learn that what I was taught in "Progressions" was based on a body of published, public knowledge that revealed the principles of the process for creation and universal law. "Progressions," I learned, was not a unique, one of a kind, class but merely a presentation of what had been already known, but not widely disseminated, for thousands of years.

As part of my self-education over the years, I've read many books on the subject of metaphysics and human capability. I have chosen not to follow the traditional academic justification paradigm used by many authors in which each concept is justified with lengthy discussions of other research that supports the authors' conclusions. In my opinion, this only lengthens the book, muddles the issues and makes the concepts they wish to present hard to grasp. So, for the sake of clarity and brevity, I have chosen not to do this. Instead, I will rely on the experience the reader has when using the process contained in this book to validate the information presented.

Of the many books I have read, there are two books on the subject of self-improvement that I feel are important to the beginning student. They are important works that are readily available and embody, from slightly different perspectives, the concepts that I present here. I highly recommend: *Think and Grow Rich* by Napoleon Hill and

Psychocybernetics by Dr. Maxwell Maltz M.D. Reading these books will substantiate what I have written here and help you in accepting your birthright and establishing your claim to a successful life.

CHAPTER ONE

The Gift of Creativity

*W*hat do you intend to do with your life? What will your future be like? Do you have personally meaningful goals and a workable plan for achieving them? If you're like most people, you don't. Either you don't know what you want, or you have a long list of material things you wish you had and goals you hope to accomplish someday but no clear plan of how to attain them. If that is so, this book is for you. The following chapters explain, in plain and simple terms, a process for identifying and achieving all your goals. If you learn and use this process, you can have anything in life you feel you deserve.

Most people don't realize that the ability to define personal goals and make them come to life lies well within the capabilities of all human beings. The ability to identify and attain our goals is encompassed by the power of creativity. "Creativity" is a term I use to describe the human ability to cause events to happen and does not refer exclusively to artistic ability. Your power to create was developed within you at the time of your conception along with the rest of your human capabilities. The ability to create your goals is innate and as instinctive as any of your other senses and not any more unusual than your sense of sight or touch. All people, whether they know it or not, are creative not just those with a special talent.

The ability to define your personal goals and create a way to make them real is an every day event that may seem magical to the uninitiated but is not magic in any way. Creativity is an ordinary, everyday ability like closing your eyes and remembering what you did last summer. In order for you to become creative and begin living a successful life, you must reacquaint yourself with your creative ability and teach yourself that your personal creativity is an attainable possibility. Once you teach yourself that you have command of your creative power you can develop it through practice.

Look at creativity this way: Everyone knows that if you want well-developed muscles, you must follow a regimen of exercise and nutrition that enables them to develop. Everyone knows that with consistent effort, the muscle building process will work, but not everyone is willing to devote the time and effort. The process for developing your creative, goal-defining and achievement ability is like the muscle-building ability. It is a straightforward process that will work, but only if you use it.

What is the basis of our creative powers; where do they come from? Creative power is a natural application of what is called universal law and will be discussed in great detail in the coming chapters. Learning how to make the universal laws work for you is the goal of this book. Once you learn this process, you can apply the laws to your goals and create a wonderful life for yourself.

To create what you want, you must first discover exactly what it is you want. Your desires and your goals are inextricably interwoven with your self-image. Your self-image is the collection of ideas, images and feelings that reflect your honest opinion of yourself. Your self-image tells you what you know you truly deserve, way down deep inside, not just what you think you ought to have coming to you.

Many people are unaware of their self-image and therefore have goals and that are not even remotely connected to their capabilities. It is not uncommon to see people struggling to be and have things their current abilities do not equip them to achieve. Not having the capability to accomplish a goal does not prevent you from achieving it. But, since all goals come with requirements, often the achievement of a goal will have to be put on hold while you develop the required abilities.

How to assess your current abilities and match them with the ability to achieve a goal will be discussed in great detail in the following chapters. But basically, once you learn how to make universal law work for you, you can apply the laws to your goals and make an accurate assessment of the direction you need to go to achieve them.

For example, if your goal is to climb Mount Everest, you cannot do so in poor physical condition. However, even if you are in poor physical condition, you can still hope to climb Mount Everest. But first you will have to change your physical conditioning to match up with the requirements of the goal of climbing Everest. You can change yourself and accomplish a goal that is presently out of reach, or you can stay as you are and accomplish goals that are more within your current capabilities. The goal determines the requirements. You must decide whether or not you want to meet them. As always, you have the choice: into the gym and on to Everest, or back to the den, the couch and the television. Either decision is fine; it's up to you to decide.

This brings up the question, what you really want, what is most important to you? What are you willing to work for and what are you willing to do to achieve your goal? Is climbing Everest really that important? The best way to find out is to establish a dialogue with your inner self at the subconscious level.

The communication with your inner self, or "subconscious" as it is called, is the starting point of all meaningful personal development because the subconscious is where your personal desires and life goals originate. The assumption made here is that at any point in your life you already know what you really want. What you lack is the realization of two points: first, that your inner self has already set goals, and second, that you already possess a way to achieve them. This pre-established inner guidance system may seem unusual at first. But if you think about it, you'll realize that all living creatures, insects, fish, birds and mammals, are born with the complete ability to live their lives. They are born knowing what to do and how to do it, and so are you.

Many people fool themselves by acting on an emotional impulse generated in their conscious mind and defending the action by saying it came from their true heart of hearts located in their subconscious mind. Self-deception of this nature is common but avoidable. The main thrust of this book is to teach you a process so that you can establish a dialogue with your inner self in such a way as to be sure that the goals you set out to achieve accurately represent your heart's true desire.

While you may intellectually agree with the idea of inborn, natural ability you are probably not convinced that it resides within you in amounts sufficient to guide your life. Like many other people, you want to believe in your self but are not sure you should; you need proof! Just imagine what a relief it would be for you to know for certain what you should be doing with your life.

Reading stories about others who have achieved greatness using the process described in the following chapters will never be enough for you. After all, other people's achievements, while they may be interesting, are irrelevant because they belong to them and speak of their powers, not yours. So, because they have no real value to you, I have left them out whenever possible. Instead, I have concentrated my discussion to the process that will provide your own personal experiences. This is the only sure way to end your doubt.

Even though the process for goal definition and achievement will be clearly laid out, with all justifications completely revealed, you will still need to experience the process yourself if you expect to benefit from it. Just reading about it is not enough. Therefore, you will be encouraged to apply the process to a simple short-term goal and gain the experience of success for yourself. You will be amazed by how easy, effective and rewarding the process is. And, with a small achievement to awaken your confidence, you will be empowered to take on bigger projects.

Even at a beginner's level, you will be astonished at what will happen. If you use the process steadily for a month you will develop an entirely new approach to life. Your new approach will enable you to begin to live your life in tune with your deepest desires. You will set and achieve goals in a way that you never thought possible. When the chains of uncertainty and doubt no longer drag you down, your head will be clear and your entire force of energy will be freed to accomplish your goals. This sense of direction and focused energy will be available to you in amounts you never thought possible.

Bringing order and harmony to your life and acquiring the material objects you desire will require work on your part, but the process described in the chapters to come has proved infallible for centuries dating back to the origins of humankind. I know this still seems too good to be true. But ask yourself: "What if it is true, what if I really can direct my life just the way I want?" Wouldn't that be absolutely excellent? You bet it would, and the only way to find out is to read this book all the way through and practice what you learn.

You have no reason to trust me now but take a chance and trust yourself. This process, in my opinion, is much easier than building bigger muscles. Take heart. If you are one of the millions of people who feel a sense of powerlessness and yearns to take control of your life, the power you seek is before you now, right in your hands!

CHAPTER TWO

Accepting the Creative Process

T he creative process goes on within us every day of our lives because the power of creativity is essential to life. To create a successful life, one must become aware of the creative process already working within and take conscious control of the results. The ability to know who you are and what you want is the foundation for the conscious creation of a successful life. Taking control of power within you requires a span of quiet time to imagine what you want. This period of quiet time is usually not more than a half-hour per day. During this time you can turn away from everyday stresses and pressures of life and reflect on what you have and plan for what you want.

To begin to understand the use of the process of creativity you must learn about the fundamental energy that makes up the universe and everything in it. This is necessary because the ability to create the conditions and circumstances of our life arises from our ability to manipulate the fundamental energy of the universe. Make no mistake: you will be involved with learning about a powerful force that can create both good and bad depending upon how you use it. And because you will want to use it for your benefit, some prior knowledge is essential.

What is this fundamental energy and what is it made of? The existence of the basic energy of the universe has been known for thousands of years. The force has been given many names over the centuries. Ancient Greek physicists and, at about the same time, scholars in the subcontinent of Asia, now called India, wrote of a force of primal matter that created the universe.

To arrive at the concept of the primal matter they reasoned back through the composition of physical matter, and intellectually divided and re-divided matter into smaller and smaller pieces. They continued this mental division until they arrived at a fundamental substance, one that could be divided no further. It was this theoretical fundamental substance that formed the basis for all other things on earth.

The Greeks called this fundamental substance the "Atomos," or that which could not be further divided. Indian scholars using the same method called it "Paramanu." The Indian scholars said this was the prime substance of creation. It was this substance that provided the foundation for all objects and experiences in the world.

In order to demystify the concept of an all powerful, amorphous omni-present energy that fills every nook and cranny of the universe, I simply call it "peanut butter." Admittedly the words "Atomos" or "Paramanu" sound more sophisticated, but peanut butter, because it is less awesome and more familiar, expresses the concept as I am presenting it.

If we were talking together instead of reading this book you would undoubtedly ask, "If there is such a thing as peanut butter, are you saying that if we use the process that we are about to learn about that we will be able to change the peanut butter into anything we want?" The answer is: "Yes you can. I do it all the time and so can you."

CHAPTER THREE

Desire, the Energy of Change

*I*t is an indisputable fact that, at some point in our lives, all of us want to become, or change into, something different or something better than we are now. We want something we consider more important, more interesting or more fulfilling. And, when we achieve the things we desire we consider ourselves successful.

The concept of desire should, at this point, be made separate from our basic, animal needs. Our discussion here is focused on our wants or what we desire not our needs. Humans, like all animals have needs. But human beings have sophisticated desires that far exceed the life-needs of living organisms. We need water but we want decaffeinated coffee; we need food but we want chocolate cake.

Realizing our desires requires us to change. What we want and how we want to change is specific to the individual. However, it is a undeniable fact of life that all of us want to become something more than we are now and must be willing to change to realize what we desire.

The desire to be something different can cause conflicts because we must undergo personal change to achieve it. Many people resist the need to change and thus are at odds with their desire to be something better. It is one of life's greatest paradoxes that you cannot want more and different things in your life without also expecting your life to change. Humans, unlike any other creature, can accept change, if they want to, in order to have more than they need to survive.

The fact that humans want a lot from life is evident in how we live it. We all have desires, hopes for the future, and material things we want to have. We want a new car even when the old car still runs great. We want bigger houses even when our present house is more than adequate for our needs. We want the latest clothes even when those we have serve us perfectly well.

The concept of desire is so intrinsic to the nature of humankind that it seems logical to conclude that the emotion of desire is essential to being human. Even if we acquire that which we once thought was the best, we will still want something more; something we perceive to be even better. No matter how much we may have now, our desire to have more is insatiable.

The dynamic motivation provided by our emotion of desire leads us to an important question. The question may seem a little strange because our desire to want more is so deeply entrenched within us. But nonetheless the question needs to be asked. The question is: Why do humans want things? Why do we want more than we need? What is the cause of our seemingly insatiable desire?

The answer can only be that we want things because at some deep level of our selves we know we can have them. Wanting something does not ensure we will get it because there is more to having something than merely wanting it. But within the concept of desire, that is wishing for or deeply wanting something, exists the mechanism for attaining it. Why else would we even think of wanting something if we couldn't have it? What would be the purpose of our desire if not to attain the object of our desire?

The answer to the question involves the assumption that like all other creatures, our human makeup is not haphazard, and we are purposefully and precisely constructed in all aspects. Much of our construction is physical in nature and inherited from our evolutionary past: We have lungs so we can breathe air, hands with thumbs so we can grasp, and internally warmed blood so we can achieve our objectives in all areas of the Earth.

But we have more than physiological capabilities; we also have vast psychological powers too. It is these psychological abilities that allow us to fulfill, or actualize, our desires. It follows, therefore, that the capacity to want more than we need to survive satisfies a deep need in all humans. The answer to why we want the extra things, not just necessary things, must be that the capacity to want something is inseparably accompanied by our ability to attain it. In other words, our desire to want things is evidence of our power to create them.

We are human because we have an intrinsic ability to create what we want. If we view our life from the perspective of our creative ability, we will see that most of life is spent manufacturing reasons to create beyond fulfillment of what we need for survival. This aspect of humankind sets us distinctly apart from animals and best defines our uniqueness as humans.

CHAPTER FOUR

Points of Explanation

*B*efore you read on, I must caution you on three points. First, there will never be a mathematical, logical, conventional proof of what you are about to learn. The information about to be presented cannot be understood solely by conventional thinking. Mathematics and logic arise from laws of the universe, not the other way around. The only way to demonstrate the validity of the laws and the process described in this book is to use them.

Some methods, even though they seem to defy logic based, conventional explanations work anyway. It is like the aeronautical engineer who studied bumblebees and concluded that according to the principles of aerodynamics, bumblebees couldn't fly. Fortunately, the bumblebees didn't know they couldn't fly and flew whenever they need to not realizing they shouldn't be able to. If the bumblebees can do it, so can you; you don't need anyone's permission. Don't worry if the laws and processes are different than what you have experienced so far. Just do what the bumblebees do. Go through the process and trust that the desired result will take place; it will.

Second, what comes next is like a puzzle. The process has many interlocking pieces, and no single part is more important than any other. When you read this book, make a serious pact with yourself *to read every word*. <u>Read the con-tents from start to finish before you practice any of the processes</u>. It's important to have an overall picture in your mind of what you want to accomplish before you begin learning the process. Once you have a feel for where the material is going, go back and do the exercises in the order they are presented. This will make the learning process easier and more effective. Take your time, be patient with your-self, and go through the exercises with an eye to mastering each one before you move on.

Third, remember that application of the process you are about to learn takes work. Life is designed to be a develop-mental process for humankind and there really isn't any such thing as a free lunch. If you want to take charge of your creativity and have a successful life you must be will-ing to work for what you want.

CHAPTER FIVE

The Laws of the Universe

*T*he laws that direct the fundamental operation of the universe have been the subjects of speculation and study throughout the ages. Many authors have arrived at seemingly different conclusions about the number and scope of these fundamental laws. The difference of opinion can be attributed to the authors' different cultures and points of view. Many authors have rather long lists of fundamental laws. Others who have delved deeper into the subject have arrived at the conclusion that there is ultimately only one law.

There have been many names for the source of this ultimate power. Some say this ultimate source of power is God or the Godhead. Others say it is love. Some combine the two words and say that God is love, and that love is the fundamental law of the universe. No matter what you call it, there is general agreement that all things come from one, all-powerful source.

The idea of one all-powerful source gives rise to many other interpretations of how the universe works. Some state the ultimate single law that arises from this one source of power and rules everything else is the law of attraction. From this perspective, our thoughts create our life by attracting to us those things we think about. The Roman

Marcus Aurelius expressed this idea long ago when he said, "Our life is what our thoughts make it."

Even though I am comfortable with the law of attraction, my observation on how the world works on the day-to-day basis requires inclusion of the concept of duality. Here on earth in the every day world, concepts are observed to have two contrasting aspects or what is known as duality. It is true that most philosophies say that the apparent duality of creation is an illusion because behind the veil of life's physical realm, all things are one. Norman MacLean eloquently expresses the idea of oneness in his work, *A River Runs Through It*. He wrote, "Eventually all things merge into one and a river runs though it." He was describing the oneness of the universe as a ceaseless flowing river of energy.

The philosophers who believe in oneness are, in my opinion, absolutely correct. But, as we function in our everyday life, we humans need mental boundaries and contrasts to define our thoughts. In order to understand our actions in our every day world, we set up the convention that creates contrasting limits. These limits define most everything we know of into two extremes. So when we think about the concepts of human experience in the everyday sense, we conceive of them as being black or white, above or below, up or down, sour or sweet, male or female, and so on. We do this so that we can work with the concept. After all, what would the word good mean if we did not have its opposite, bad, to act as its opposite, defining point? The conceptual duality provides the extremes of contrast and a midpoint of balance that helps us understand our worlds.

While the duality of concepts, as I call it, does not deny the ultimate reality of omnipresent, dynamic energy, it does not dwell on it. So, because it is much easier for us to understand, I use two laws to describe the universe even though they do it in less than ultimate terms.

15

Therefore, for purposes of our discussion, the laws of the universe come as a pair. These two laws govern all existence, all creation, all thoughts and all material objects. The laws have always been in existence; they were a part of the process of the creation of the universe. The two laws are: the Law of Consciousness and the Law of Return.

CHAPTER SIX

The Law of Consciousness

*T*he first law of the universe is the Law of Consciousness. For sake of brevity this law will be referred to as Law I. The Law of Consciousness says: *Whatever you hold in consciousness as being truly real for you is or becomes real.* This law is deceptively simple and requires more discussion before you accept it.

What do I mean by consciousness? Consciousness is the totality of your thoughts, knowledge, experience, feelings and awareness. As used in this context, the term "thought" refers to mental images, concepts and visions you experience as you go through day-to-day life. Everyday thoughts are responses to immediate stimuli from the outside world AND the result of mental activity at a deep, creative level of mind. The Law of Consciousness operates primarily through thoughts that are held deep within our mind.

For most people, the first impression of Law I is that it seems vague and open-ended. Does the law mean that my thoughts actually become real physical objects? The answer is an emphatic yes. Thoughts that are retained in your mind long enough to become clear mental images can, and often do, become real.

"Wait a minute," you say. "I never saw the Rocky Mountains until last summer and I didn't have a mental image of them as they really are until I saw them. So how could I have created them?" The answer is, of course, that you didn't create them. The Rocky Mountains were created as a result of tectonic forces in the earth's crust that were set in motion by the creator of the Earth.

What you experienced when you saw the Rocky Mountains was the result of another consciousness's creation. The interactions of your personal experiences and creations, and the results of the creations of other consciousnesses make up the totality of your life experiences. Just how you and all the other creative beings on the planet interact can get a bit confusing and needs some careful explaining.

There are two aspects of creation that are equally important to your life experience. First there are aspects of your life that you literally create for yourself. For example, you might want to become a college graduate, and your creativity and hard work over time creates the reality of a completed course of college level study. Or, you may want to have something that is already created but it is something you do not presently have in your life. For example let's say it is a new, red car.

Will you personally, actually create the car? No, workers who used plans and machinery built the car in a factory. All you did was create the space for a red car in your life. You created the space and means to own the car by the thoughts you held in consciousness.

This second aspect of creation leads to an important question. What is the point of creating something from the ground up that is already created? If you think about it, all you really want is the use of the things you want. You don't really want to reinvent the wheel when you want to know what time it is, do you? Of course you don't. However, if the thing you want has not been created yet, like a new invention, a piece of art or literature, or an original solution

18

to a problem, you can create that by envisioning the result you need. The vast majority of things that people want exist ready to use or exist in a form that only requires minor modification to suit our specific needs. Make no mistake; you can actually create what you want from the peanut butter of the universe. But, in most cases, you don't need to. All you need to create is a space for the things you want in your life.

The second aspect of creation, things that are created by others, gives rise to another important issue. The issue is the reaction in your mind; good/bad, love it/hate it, to the things created by other people's consciousnesses. Any situation or object created by someone else can be wonderful or terrible depending upon how you react to it. How you perceive an object or event, creates your personal reality in any given situation. The phrase "perception is reality" is one of the foundation blocks of psychology and is a common interpretation of reality.

So, in the case of the Rocky Mountains you didn't actually make them, you just experienced the results of someone else's creation. You had to have a general mental picture of mountains already, or you wouldn't have known what those huge, snow covered humps in the earth were. Your personal reality contained a vision of mountains, but it did not contain the refined vision of the Rocky Mountains you received when you visited them.

Your personal reality changed as you became more aware of the condition of the Rockies. Your personal reaction to them depended upon the conditions and circumstances of your life. Personal reality, all reality for that matter, is not a static situation. As you grow more aware, your personal reality changes to accept your new state of awareness. A brief discussion of reality will help you to understand.

19

The reality of the world can be thought of as a kaleido-scope, a dynamic mosaic that moves in response to all activities of the earth and all of its inhabitants. The life you create out of this mosaic of activity is your own personal reality. Your present reality is based upon your own awareness, environment, perceptions and expectations. Your personal reality, or your world as it is commonly called, is a mixture of your personal creations, and your reaction to the creations and reactions of all others. You don't react to everything in your world. But you pick and choose aspects of the reality around you. Your choices, what you react to or don't react to it form your life. What you react to depends largely on what and who you think should be part of your life.

Think of your world as if you were an artist visiting a huge art gallery. In the gallery you see paintings you painted and paintings by many others. Of course, you like all of your paintings and some of the other paintings as well, but you don't like them all. As you wander through this large gallery you realize you will not have time to see it all, but nonetheless you acquire a general impression of whether or not you like the gallery overall. Your reaction to the art gallery is based upon your individual makeup, what you saw in the gallery, and what your education and value systems allow you to think is appropriate. You think or, should I say, assume that every other person who comes to the gallery will have about the same experience as you. In general, you will be right. But other visitors will have their own reactions based upon their own expectations, prior experiences and their reaction to the reality they perceive. Some people won't like your paintings just as you don't like someone else's paintings.

Most people agree to a large extent to what the realities of life are; helping people is good, stealing is bad, the Grand

Canyon is awesome, and so on. Yet within the wide area of opinion on any issue, there is usually much room for disagreement because all humans are different. Even the Rocky Mountains can create different realities in different people. To the long-haul truck driver in the icy, cold of winter, the Rocky Mountains become a test of endurance and driving ability. To the snow skier, the Rocky Mountains become a place to ski and enjoy the beauty of nature in winter. The place is the same, the weather conditions are the same, but the experience of the trucker and the skier are very different. The difference in perception is due to the individual reaction to the existing conditions.

The reality of the entire world, or the global reality as it is called, is created by the combination of the activities of the earth itself, the activities of each person on the planet, and our reactions to those activities. The sum total of all these realities results in what is called the group consciousness. It is the group consciousness, or the aggregate of all thoughts and activities plus everyone's reactions to those activities, that determines the reality of the world.

When discussing reality, it is important to remember that reality has a broad meaning. It involves not only physical things but also mental things like thoughts and dreams. In most people's understanding of reality, a mental vision, a thought, an image or a dream only seems partially real. A vision is not considered to be real, though it should be, because the vision has no substance to it. It is "all in our head" so to speak. Most people consider real things to have physical properties like mass and volume. But since thoughts and feelings don't have physical properties they are considered less than real. This is a common but very misleading perception. This false perception must be put aside if you are to take control of your creativity. Creativity is a capability that is easier to experience than understand because there are many unseen forces at work in the world.

As you will learn, the world in many ways is not as it appears at all. Tangible objects are not as solid as they seem. Our belief in their permanence is what creates their durability. On the other hand, intangible objects such as visions, emotions and dreams are not as insubstantial as they seem. As we all know, emotions and feelings can have a very direct and powerful effect on how we feel and react. In actuality, at the most fundamental levels of existence, all things, tangible and intangible, are equally real because they are composed of the same thing, the peanut butter. All things have at their origin unthinkably small quantities of vibrating energy that occupy relatively vast areas of empty space. In order to understand this, a quick explanation is required of how matter is constructed.

CHAPTER SEVEN

The Nature of Matter

K nowledge of the fundamental nature of matter will help us accept our ability to create. To understand our power of creativity we need to understand the true nature of matter; especially the realities of solid, tangible matter. The following discussion will link your understanding of solid matter with your creative power and will provide a basis of acceptance of your power to create.

In the normal, everyday understanding of our world, we think of all the objects and substances that exist as being composed of various forms of solid, tangible matter. But, if we take even a basic course in physical science we learn that matter is not just solid but actually exists in four states, or phases, that describe the matter in various degrees of density. The least dense phase is plasma, the next is gaseous, the next is liquid and the last, and most dense is solid. But even "solid" matter is not as solid as it appears.

Solid matter is actually composed of infinitesimal amounts of vibrating energy that is contained by electrical attraction in a vast amount of space. To understand this let's consider a hydrogen atom. A hydrogen atom is the simplest form of immutable matter and is composed of two basic subatomic particles. The center, or nucleus, contains one particle of positively charged, vibrating energy called a proton.

The second particle, called an electron, is a speck of vibrating energy located outside the nucleus. An electron has a negative charge that attracts it to the proton. A proton and an electron attracted to each other make up a hydrogen atom.

Both the proton and the electron are very small. *Ten billion* protons laid end to end would measure only one meter (39.37 inches) in length. And an electron is nearly two thousand times (1/1836th) *smaller* than a proton. Electrons, by the way, are not stationary but are thought to occupy distinct energy levels at a relatively great distance from the nucleus. The distance between the proton and the electron, though actually very small, has been compared to the distance from the earth to the sun.

So, when we think of physical matter as being solid, we should remember that empty space is the largest part of the volume of any object. Objects become tangible because the atoms from which they are constructed are packed together and overlaid on one another in such vast quantities that they form a network that results in the characteristics of that particular phase of matter. Even a stone, as solid as it seems, is composed of 99.9% open space. Look at it this way: A person can stand on a bridge made of chain link fence even though the fence is actually 10% solid matter and 90% percent open space.

But in order to have a solid acceptance for our power to create, we must investigate subatomic particles even more closely and travel intellectually to the very heart of existence. Because even though subatomic particles are very small, there are other, even smaller, particles that makes up the "bigger" subatomic particles.

Scientists who study the properties of subatomic particles are called particle physicists. They work along with quantum mechanic mathematicians in a highly technical world at the junction of science and philosophy. To understand the construction of the atom, particle physicists seek to discover the number and characteristics of the building block particles that make up the subatomic particles.

Subatomic particles are all alike and are found in all atoms. To explore the construction of subatomic particles scientists use huge devices called cyclotrons. A cyclotron is a symmetrical, circular tunnel about a mile in diameter. Devices that generate strong, pulsating magnetic fields surround the cyclotron. Scientists introduce subatomic particles into the cyclotron and use the pulsing of the magnetic force fields to accelerate the particles to speeds approaching the speed of light. Once the particles are whizzing in one direction, the scientists introduce other subatomic particles going in the opposite direction. Their intent is to create collisions that will cause the particles to break apart.

The collisions are difficult to arrange and data is hard to obtain because the results of this cosmic crashing last only a fragment of a second. What these scientists hope to discover are the properties of the pieces that result when these subatomic particles collide. Imagine crashing a bowling ball into a jet airplane flying at high speed in order to break the jet plane into its individual pieces, then trying to discover how many different pieces the plane contains. Fortunately, atoms contain fewer pieces than jet planes.

So particles that are traveling very fast collide with other particles going in the opposite direction. The collision of these particles reveals the even smaller particles that make up the subatomic particles. As a result of this experimentation, particle physicists have identified a dozen or so subatomic particles infinitesimally smaller than electrons that make up the "big" subatomic particles. Quantum mechanics mathematicians now theorize that the most fundamental particles of the physical universe are constructed of incomprehensibly small, vibrating "strings" of matter. Theoretically, the frequency of the string's vibration ultimately gives rise to the matter that it constructs.

We don't need a cyclotron to break down matter; we can use our intellect to mentally divide matter and come to the same conclusion. As we divide subatomic particles into their separate components, they must become smaller and smaller until all their parts have been identified and those smaller parts have been further divided until more division is not possible. Historians have credited the ancient Greek physicist Democritus with doing this intellectual division in the fifth century B.C. using his powers of reason; Democritus deduced that the final division of matter would reveal what he described as a "primal mass in everlasting motion." Democritus called this vibrating, primal mass the "atomos," which means that which is indivisible. The modern term "string" and the ancient term "atomos" both can be used as an equivalent to my term, the peanut butter.

When modern scientists ultimately arrive at that point of indivisibility where no more subatomic particles can be identified, only vibrating energy, the peanut butter, will be left. The peanut butter will have been revealed by use of the scientific method rather than by the use of pure reason. Then the particle physicists and quantum mechanics mathematicians will have demonstrated scientifically what the Greek physicist Democritus reasoned intellectually 2,500 years ago.

Both methods of investigation, philosophy and science, take us to the same place but by different paths. In the final analysis, both methods will agree on the result, which is the existence of the peanut butter. It does not matter how we arrive at the basic concept of the essence of matter because in either proof, whether through science or philosophy, one final question remains: Of what substance is the peanut butter made?

CHAPTER EIGHT

The Illusion Reality

*W*hat lies beyond the peanut butter, the vibrating, and omnipresent, primal energy of the
universe? Using the scientific process alone,
science can never answer the question. When solving questions, science requires the use of the scientific method. Therefore, in order to conduct a proper scientific investigation,
science must expect to find a tangible substance or some
tangible effect. And beyond the peanut butter - the primal,
vibrating, all pervasive energy of the universe is - **nothing,** -
nothing at all. In the final analysis, the ancient philosophers
were right because ultimately nothing is real, and everything is an illusion created by shimmering masses of energy
in everlasting motion.

How and why the universe was created from nothing
and the nothing created into peanut butter is not known.
The only conclusion that can be drawn is that the totality
of tangible reality, our entire universe, is ultimately based
on the activity of a creative consciousness. The nature and
desires of this creative consciousness is the subject of all religions and not this book.

However, as we shall see, for reasons unknown to me,
we humans are invited to participate in acts of creation. Our
creative powers are only limited by our imagination and or
desire to do the work necessary to make them manifest.

This essential fact is our birthright; yet it is unknown by the vast majority of humankind.

Even though we ordinary folk can manipulate the peanut butter, the scientific reason for this capability has never been uncovered. The fact that science has not yet proved why we can create is of no consequence. Natural phenomena do not require scientific proof for their existence. Fledgling birds do not need the principle of flight proved to them before they fly. They flap their wings instinctively and, when they are strong enough, take to the sky. They fly for the rest of their life and never know why they can.

It will be the same for you. Try the process I am about to describe a couple of times and prove to yourself you can do it. You will be able to create a successful life even if you never fully believe that everything in the world is ultimately an illusion and exists solely as a result of the activity of a creative consciousness.

Even though matter is ultimately an illusion, it is best not to get carried away with the idea as you live your life day to day. Illusions can become very real and take on substantial concreteness. If you step in front of a speeding taxicab, you will get flattened even if it is, in the final analysis, only an illusion.

To complete the foundation for Law I, The Law of Consciousness, we must next consider the opposite of tangible matter. We must consider the tangibility of seemingly intangible things: the mental images, visions and dreams that arise from stimulation of nerves in the brain. How can images we have in our mind, images that have no physical properties, create tangible elements in our lives? To understand the creative force of images on tangible matter, we must develop an understanding of how mental images are created.

CHAPTER NINE

The Nature of Thought

*M*ental images are a result of highly complex nerve interactions responding to stimuli from outside and inside the brain. In the final analysis, all brain stimuli are nothing more than extremely small charges of peanut butter-like waveform energy operating at different levels of intensity. Scientists calculate the intensity of waveform energy by measuring how frequently the wave peaks pass a measuring point in one second. Different intensity levels have different intervals between wave peaks. The time intervals between the wave peaks are called frequencies. It is the interaction of different energy frequencies with the nerve endings in our sense organs that produce nerve impulse signals of different intensity that are transferred to the brain.

For things we see, these different signals from the stimulated nerves in our eyes are transmitted to the brain via the optic nerve. In the brain the signals combine in the vision center to create pictures within our mind. In other words, the nerve impulses received by your eyes are assembled by your brain's vision center to create a picture of the energy fluctuations that are picked up by your eyes. The brain interprets low frequency signals as the color red, while higher frequency signals are interpreted as the color violet. All the colors of the rainbow lie between the colors red and violet, and are only minute variations in the frequency of reflected light. In actuality, millions of signals bombard the brain each second. The signals are different energy frequencies picked up by the energy receptors of your five senses: ears, eyes, nose, tongue, and touch located throughout your body.

Our brain's reaction to the bombardment it receives from these sensors creates our perception of the world around us. Our brain's most dramatic reactions to stimuli are the formation of mental pictures. The mental pictures are not only organized recollections of the various energy frequencies received by our sensors but also representations of the deepest desires in our mind. An understanding of ability to create mental pictures is essential to acceptance of our power of creation.

Mental pictures can arise from stimuli received from outside the brain, as in the case of the eyes and the other four senses, or from within the brain itself as a result of the self-stimulating capacity of the brain. The internal source of picture-forming stimuli arises from the fact that we can use one part of our brain to produce mental pictures in another part. These internally generated mental pictures are called dreams, emotions, visions or feelings. We can see images of what is outside our bodies by opening our eyes, or we can "see" what is outside our bodies by closing our eyes and visualizing in our mind what is out there. Both processes produce images we see in our mind.

Our normal reaction is to classify the open eyed, external stimulation as more valuable than the internal stimulation. We believe what is outside ourselves is physically tangible and therefore more "real" than what is inside our mind. We have been taught to put greater faith and value on what we see with our eyes open than what we visualize in our mind with our eyes closed. In everyday life, the faith in and value of a chair as a comfortable place to sit is better if it is a tangible object that will support our backside rather than a vision. However, in the world of creative consciousness, internally generated visions are very real and very important.

By the way, our eyes are not the only conduits for generating visions in the brain. All of our other senses can do the same thing. For example, hearing soft, pleasing sounds, smelling a pie baking, or the old comforting feel of a texture of fabric that reminds us of our childhood blanket can create a vision of home and a feeling of peace and tranquility within us. All visions are important to creativity no matter what sense gives rise to the vision.

The importance of visions arises from the fact that the power of your creative consciousness can shape the peanut butter into whatever you want. When creating your life, your mind's visions are your guide. In the most fundamental sense, the basic energy needed to stimulate the optic neurons in the vision center of your brain, eyes open or eyes shut, comes from the vibrating energy of the peanut butter. The basic energy that creates an intangible vision or emotion is part of the same basic energy that creates a physical object. At the most fundamental level of existence, the vast array of emotions of which humans are capable is just as "real" as tangible matter. Remember, both tangible matter and intangible matter at their point of origin are constructed of the same fundamental energy- the peanut butter -transformed by the desires of creative consciousness.

If you have trouble understanding this, you are considering the problem at the everyday level of mind. At the everyday level, a concrete sidewalk really is harder than a dream. Diving off your roof onto the pavement and holding a vision that the concrete will turn to water before you hit is not a good idea. But remember, everything that humankind has ever built has resulted from a plan that is the result of an idea or vision first held within the mind. Without an inner vision to guide you, you could not create anything or understand anything. You might be able to know about something but you wouldn't truly understand it. You would be like my students who, after a long, and what I thought was a beautifully prepared, discussion on atomic theory and the structure of matter, have the courage to raise their hands and say, "Mr. Tillman, I don't get it!" What don't they get? They don't get the picture, the vision, of what I am saying. Without the vision they can't understand or use the information. Visions are the first step in creation and essential to human progress.

The point of this discussion of matter and visions is this. By the use of Law I, the Law of Consciousness, *you can manipulate basic energy of the universe, the peanut butter, into what you think you deserve. But you must deal with it at the most fundamental level, before it becomes concrete like the pavement.*

The process used to do this will be explained in detail in Chapter Twenty-Three. But for now, what is necessary is that you understand that Law I makes this possible. In fact, you already manipulate basic energy into reality but you are not aware of the process you are using to make it happen. For example, consider the parking place angel.

I believe it is common knowledge, especially with supershoppers, that if you want a parking place near the door of the mall, all you have to do is "picture" a vacant place near the entrance in your mind as you drive into the parking lot, and one will be there for you. The parking place angel works things out so that a convenient place is available when you get there.

Did your mind make the car that was there disappear? Did the angel make the other shopper's children suddenly tired and cranky, forcing a quick exit? Not likely, yet the parking place was there for you just the way you knew it would be. Was a new parking place created just for you? Or was the parking place vacant just by chance? Does it really matter why it was there? You wanted a parking space and it was there for you. By the way, if you think the parking space was there by chance, it was. But if you think it was there because of you envisioned a short walk to the mall door, then that's why it was there. In either case Law I is validated. The only thing difference between these two examples is the person's reaction to the reason for the vacant parking place.

The example of the parking place angel can raise as many questions as it answers. We could spend years discussing the various possibilities of why the parking space was there and still not resolve the issue. No matter what we conclude, the fact remains that the space is there for those who know it will be.

Take heart, the process presented in the following chapters will allow you the opportunity to become consciously creative on a much more specific and personal level. The process will be explained in detail and you will have no doubts about your ability to control your creative powers. Before we get into that, however, it is essential that we discuss the second law of the universe, the Law of Return.

CHAPTER TEN

The Law of Return

*T*he Law of Return says: ***Whatever you hold in consciousness, as being true for you and others, is what you receive.*** The Law of Return, or Law II, is the perfect balance to the Law of Consciousness. A simpler way to think of Law II is: What you give out is what you get back. The law, like the first law, is deceptively simple and needs careful explanation.

Law II, The Law of Return, supports the vast power contained in Law I. Law II provides a feedback mechanism for the thoughts humans hold in consciousness. The law acts as a mirror, and ideally a buffer, to the creative power available in Law I. The source of the laws, whatever that might be, provides a vast power that, given the self-centered nature of most humans, requires a control. Law II is the balance and control needed for the power contained in Law I.

Implied in Law II is the fact that there can never be a double standard for the application of Law II. Whatever we think in our heart, as being good for ourselves and others is what we receive. Many people delude themselves by having two sets of thoughts. They have thoughts for what they want for themselves and thoughts they feel are good, or good enough, for others. Ultimately, there is one dominant thought, deep down, that each person applies in each situation. The possibility for abundant wealth, for example, cannot be available to some humans and not to others. In your deep consciousness, wealth is either available to all humans or to none. If you want to attain wealth you have to believe that all others can do so too, and you cannot block, physically or mentally, the possibility of them attaining it. Whether other humans actually do attain wealth is up to them. The law always applies equally to everyone.

Law II can be slow acting, but it is very effective. For example, if you practice a double standard and are honest with some people but not honest with others, you will find yourself in the company of people who are dishonest but appear to be honest and expect you to be honest too. Law II also contains a reflective element that can illuminate a self-damaging aspect of human behavior.

People who are unaware of universal law can, through their subconscious thoughts, bring on a cycle of personal unhappiness that afflicts them repeatedly. They hurt themselves without realizing that they are causing their own misfortune. They spend their energy whining about their fate and blaming others for their problems without doing anything to stop their personally created cycle of misfortune. Blaming other people for your misfortunes is like blaming the mailman for bringing you all those worrisome bills. To stop the cycle, you have to change the images you hold in your mind. Those new images will, in turn, change your actions with regard to spending money.

On the other hand, people who enjoy a good life, sound health, a satisfying job and supportive relationships are those who hold beneficial images for themselves *and others* in their mind. Law II provides that those who hold beneficial, supportive thoughts for themselves and others in their subconscious mind will receive those thoughts themselves and benefit from the support of others as they live their lives. Law

II, the Law of Returns, is nothing new. It is also called the golden rule and one of the cornerstones of all religions.

The fact that Law of Return provides a mirror of the images we maintain in our consciousness can be good news or bad news. The good news / bad news results from the fact that this mirror of ourselves, provided by Law II reflects our behavior and gives us a chance to see ourselves as we really are. What we see happening in our lives is a mirror of what we think in our hearts. This can be painful if you don't like the life or the self you see revealed.

In order to move ahead with a new, successful life you must realize that you cannot run from yourself and that you must accept personal responsibility for your life as it is now. Remember, the laws have always been in existence and didn't begin to operate just when you learned of them. Your present life, happy or troubled, is what you made it. However, the good news is that as you review the conditions and circumstances of your life, if you see things you dislike, you can use your observations as a basis for change.

As every psychologist knows, you can only change those things in your life and personality for which you feel directly responsible. So if you don't like the things you see in your life, you have to accept that that is what you created for yourself. Once you accept that what you are now is the product of your own creation, you can change yourself into a new, better you. You can do this in the privacy of your own subconscious mind, and no one needs to be the wiser.

Thankfully, the opposite is true too. If during the course of your self-examination you see good qualities, and there will be many, you can take pride in them. Most people when they evaluate themselves dwell only on the negative. If you dwell only on the negative life can become a self-depreciating slugfest and not much fun. It is important that as you investigate your life that you view yourself realistically with the many good qualities, and your faults in mind.

Self-evaluation and the changes that you want to make apply only to you and not to others. In other words, don't tell your friend that he or she looks fat to you and you think it's a good idea for him or her to lose weight just because you have decided to lose weight yourself. Those suggestions, however well meant, are seldom well received. There are, however, actions you can take to be of service to other people. Being of service means helping them to help themselves. The method for serving others will be described in the coming chapters. For now, just remember that you cannot change others, but you can help them change themselves if that is something they want to do.

Taken together, Laws I and II provide the basis for all existence. You may have whatever it is that you can imagine and believe you deserve, so long as you believe is possible for others to attain what you want for yourself. If it were not for the proviso " *What you give out is what you get back,*" humanity would quickly become a battleground of selfish interests. People could do whatever they wanted to do to other people and expect no repercussions. The strongest consciousness would ultimately win. But the winner of the battle would be the most unhappy, dissatisfied person the universe has ever known.

In the wisdom of its guiding laws, the universe has prevented us from experiencing the worst fate imaginable. What would it be like to have everything the universe has to offer and no one to share it with? Whether we can see it or not, perfection exists within the framework of the universal laws.

CHAPTER ELEVEN

The Two-Part Mind

*A*ll functions necessary for life and all actions and accomplishments are products of the interactions of the two part mind. Understanding the mind is not easy because the interactions between its two parts are unimaginably complex. To facilitate the discussion, a distinction between the brain and the mind needs to be made.

The brain is a physical object and the primary organ of the central nervous system. The brain is an organ composed of specialized nerve cells with a mass of about 5 pounds divided into two hemispheres. It is this large mass of integrated neurons that receives stimulation from the environment, stores data and regulates body functions.

The mind, on the other hand, is not as easy to define. Even though the mind is located in the brain it is not considered to be an actual, physical object. Rather it is the consciousness that results from the impressions, data, sensations, and memories stored in the brain. The mind is generally considered to be the thinking, feeling part of consciousness associated with the intellect and emotions. To complicate matters further, the mind is thought of as having two divisions; the conscious and unconscious. These two divisions will be discussed in detail later. But, essentially, the mind resides in the brain but is separate from it. The mind is the result of the information stored in the brain.

Scientists, undaunted by the complexities of the brain and mind, have begun, through careful experimentation, to unravel their interdependent operations. But despite their dedicated efforts, the mind's overall capacity and scope remain largely a mystery. However, the mind continues to function despite scientists' lack of understanding of the myriad ways it works.

If we were required to believe in only what we understood completely, our belief system would be very small. So, as we begin the exploration of the mind, do not be put off by your lack of understanding of the mind's functions. You must trust your own experiences and accept that your mind functions perfectly well without your complete understanding. You will need to let what you are able to accomplish using the process of creativity be your proof of the mind's potential.

CHAPTER TWELVE

Common Terms

*D*espite its persistent mysteries, some functions of the mind have been known for thousands of years. Scholars of the past knew that each human had a brain whose activities gave rise to the mind and spirit. Also, they knew that humans possessed a creative power that allowed them the freedom to choose the course of their lives. They knew that visualization during meditation was the most efficient path to using the creative power. The ancients predated science and did not need scientific proof to substantiate their experience any more than you need science to tell you that you need to breathe. The only proof we will have of our mental powers is our experience with them.

Before we continue our exploration of the power of the mind, especially the power of creation, we should define in everyday terms some common concepts that are used to describe the mind's function.

The conscious mind: The conscious mind provides us with the ability to know we are alive. It is the conscious mind that is in control of the day-to-day life functions such as walking, talking and doing our jobs. The conscious mind processes information from our five senses, analyzes data, considers alternatives, makes choices (shall I wear a red sweater with khaki trousers or a blue one?), and directs our body to react to immediate physical and emotional stimuli.

The conscious mind is like the screen on a computer. All the work that the computer is asked to do shows up on the screen. No one sees the millions of calculations necessary to make the screen project the computers calculations. The screen, like the conscious mind, is important as an indicator of the computer's work. But no one who knows computers thinks the screen did the work on its own; it is just a place where the unseen workings of the computer are projected.

Unconscious/Subconscious Mind: The unconscious mind conducts the planning, development and coordination of the human body. Within the subconscious mind are two divisions of effort. One directs the activities necessary to keep our bodily systems functioning such as circulation, respiration and digestion. The task of running the body's systems requires a tremendous amount of brainpower. If we had to consciously keep track of the simultaneous operation of our body systems we couldn't survive. Our conscious mind does not have enough capacity to keep up with such a task; the sheer volume of operating commands would overwhelm it. According to some authors as little as 10 percent of the minds total capacity is devoted to activities of the conscious mind. The remaining 90 percent is used is by the subconscious mind to monitor and regulate the functions of the body. The larger part of the brain is used for subconscious activities because this is where most of the work in life is done. In addition to keeping our body functioning, the subconscious mind is a storehouse of intangibles, such as creative powers, instincts, emotions, feelings, fears, fantasies and psychological programs.

Psychological Programs: A psychological program is a learned set of responses, sort of a mental shortcut, which conditions a person to feel or act, either emotionally or physically, in a predetermined way. Sometimes the conditions and circumstances that made the program useful have changed, and though the program still controls us, it may have out lived its usefulness. For example, I have a dog named Lucy. Lucy is lovable but excitable, and she will run off after the kids playing in the neighborhood if I don't keep her in the yard. To keep her in the yard I have installed an electric fence. If Lucy tries to go outside the fence, her electric collar gives her a shocking reminder of her limits. Lucy is smart. Just one shock from the collar and she will not test the limits of the fence again. Sometimes I forget to put her collar back on after I walk her but she still stays in the yard. Lucy is programmed to stop by the expectation of a shock at the boundaries of the yard and will not run off even though she could. Her prior knowledge of the force field surrounding the fence controls her action even though her collar is off and she is free to roam.

Humans can be programmed in the same way. If some people become unhappy they will want to eat even if they are not hungry. Other people program themselves to think they need a drink after work to relax. Please don't think that all psychological programs are bad; many are very necessary. For example, all mothers are programmed to protect their children. Threaten a child when mom is around and you've got big trouble with an irate mom. I am programmed to brush my teeth before going to bed. If I don't brush my teeth, I can't go to sleep. Programs can be good or bad depending upon the things they cause us to do at a particular stage of our life.

However, not all the psychological programs acquired in our youth are useful, especially in an adult mind. Overzealous adults and authority figures more concerned with controlling behavior than providing useful information implanted many programs in our childhood. For example, "Don't go out in the rain in bare feet or you'll catch a cold." Or, "If you enjoy sexual activity you will have low moral standards." Programs can be good or bad depending upon how they make us react. The subconscious contains hundreds of programs acquired in the past that affect the way we live our lives now. Recognizing that these programs exist and learning how to change them, if we want to, is one of the benefits of using the creative mind.

Awareness: The concept of awareness is often confused with consciousness. The confusion is understandable, but it is important that the difference be clarified. To be conscious of an event, say a baseball game, is to know that the game is taking place. We can hear it on the radio, see it on television, or buy a ticket and see it in person. In each instance, we are conscious of the event, but as our physical and mental proximity to the game increases our awareness increases as we experience the totality of the event.

Awareness is a heightened perception of an event of which you are conscious. When you are aware, not just conscious, you incorporate more of the information provided by your senses into the overall experience in front of you. If, for example, you want to increase your awareness of a baseball game, you attempt to recognize all aspects of the experience and absorb all of the events surrounding the game. You see the colors of the clothes on the people in the stands. You see and smell hot dogs and newly mown grass. You hear the crisp crack of the bat and the roar of the crowd. You feel the sultry air of a summer afternoon and sense the excitement in the ballpark. A full awareness of the game requires you to perceive with all your senses what is happening around you. In that way you can come to fully appreciate and enjoy the experience of which you are conscious.

Increased awareness is one of the essential elements of living a successful life. But increased awareness has a more important aspect to it. Increased awareness is also very necessary to the creative process because the answers to questions you may have about achieving your goals may come in the form of an inspiration triggered by some aspect of your surroundings and not in ways you expect. So a heightened awareness of what is happening in your life will provide you answers to questions involving your creative solutions to problems as well as making life, in general, more enjoyable.

Attachments: Another aspect of mental function is our attentiveness to the way information is stored in the unconscious mind. Information is stored in the subconscious in the form of mental impressions called attachments. An attachment is our reaction to, or conclusion about, an idea or concept used to guide our actions. Often we receive attachments from our parents, family or friends that are based on *their* interpretation of life, not ours. Some attachments, instilled when we were young, no longer work for us as adults. With a heightened awareness of information in our subconscious, we can review these attachments and change them if we choose.

For example, some people may attach the idea of acquiring wealth to the concept of happiness. Many unhappy people feel that if they had money they would be happy. As any wealthy person can tell you, money in and of itself will not make you happy. There is no doubt that having the essentials of life will contribute significantly to the feeling of well-being. However, wealth and happiness are not directly related, and having the money to buy more than the essentials of life will not automatically make you happy. If that were true, people with lots of money would be very happy, and people with no money (a native on a tropical island, for example) would be miserably unhappy. Neither statement is true. So, attaching money to happiness may result in being unhappy when there is no reason for it other than our attachment of money to happiness.

Sometimes "good" attachments need to be examined as well. For example, some people may attach physical exercise to a sense of feeling healthy and good about themselves. If they find themselves in circumstances where physical exercise is not practical - a business trip to an unfamiliar place, for example - they may experience feelings of ill health and a lack of self-worth simply because they haven't exercised. No doubt, money to provide the essentials of life and exercise is good in the overall evaluation of life. But our attachments to them may not always work to our benefit. If we endeavor to understand our attachments, we can take control of our lives and experience an increased sense of contentment, no matter what the conditions and circumstances.

Brain as a Computer: The brain is the engine of the mind. It is responsible for storing the information used by the mind in its conscious and unconscious operations. As amazing as it is, the brain is nothing more than a highly efficient computer. Like a computer, the brain has no moral direction, no sense of right and wrong. Put bad or incomplete information in a computer and you'll get bad or incomplete information out. "GIGO" as the computer experts say: garbage in, garbage out. The reverse is true of course: input good information, and good results will come out. How do we know when the information we put in is good or bad? We can check the results; if we are putting good information into our brains, then good, positive things are happening in our lives. If we have bad results, we can be sure that we have not been in-putting good information.

CHAPTER THIRTEEN

The Universal Mind

C reative problem solving requires finding new solutions to problems. The method needed to find new and unique solutions to problems brings up an interesting aspect of consciousness called the "universal mind." This aspect of consciousness is well known but not often discussed because it seems so contrary to our perceptions of everyday reality. As strange as it may seem, we have all had experiences with the universal mind. We don't discuss them much because we can't explain them. Yet they can be explained if we broaden our concept of what exists and our concept of our problem solving abilities.

Truly creative problem solving requires us to devise new solutions to the problems that confront us. As the Greek philosopher Socrates understood long ago, creative problem solving requires a storage bank of ideas that contains those solutions previously unknown to you. The ideas in the storage bank need not be completely new, but they can be. Most often the problem you face only requires a connection between the problem and a solution. The universal mind is the dimension of existence that allows us access to information that lies in a source called "universal intelligence."

Universal intelligence is best described as a pool of all knowledge contained through the ages. One of the most mysterious aspects of life is that it appears that every possibility for every action and reaction in the universe has already been thought out and already exists. The book, *The Legend of Bagger Vance* by Stephen Pressfield, deals with the pre-existence of every possibility in the context of golf. The book is an interesting source for an introduction to the universal mind. Brian Greene, author of *The Elegant Universe*, discusses the universal mind indirectly through his presentation of Richard Feynman's theories on quantum mechanics, in particular the behavior of electrons in certain situations. I mention these two dissimilar works as support for the idea of universal mind because it is the most difficult to understand of all the concepts presented in this book. I hope you will be encouraged to accept the concept if others from widely different backgrounds believe in it too. While the existence of the universal mind is hard to justify by using logic and science, it does indeed exist as you can demonstrate easily to yourself using the creative process.

The benefits of using the universal mind extend beyond problem- solving. The universal mind can also be used to communicate with others whether or not we are in their presence. We can communicate not only with human minds, but also with the minds of animals and other living things.

The universal mind sounds spookier than it really is. The truth is that we can all develop the ability to read minds if we make it a priority to do so. If you think about it for a minute, you will realize you have used the universal mind in an experience called precognition. For example, you hear the phone ring and know who the caller is before you answer. Or you know when an anticipated letter has been delivered before you open the mailbox. Or you feel the urge to contact someone and, when you do, realize they were not feeling well or unhappy and wanted to talk to you.

The universal mind also gives rise to all manner of psychic phenomena: hunches, premonitions, creative flashes, intuition, "lucky" guesses, faith healing and fortune telling. Western culture, with its over-reliance on scientific proof, tends to be leery of information retrieved from this area of consciousness. But, as we shall see, it has merit as part of an overall, creative goal-achievement process.

Enlightened people are those who have seen the "light." They understand the power of the human consciousness and the universal mind. They use their power constructively to strive to direct the course of humanity to a constructive end. They know that by being of service to humankind they, each in their own way, contribute to the betterment of the world. It is the process of service that adds their constructive efforts to the overall, world consciousness and thus improves the world.

The question that arises now is how do you, as you begin your journey to enlightenment, go about making the world a better place? The question reminds me of a lyric from an old rock song that goes, "I'd like to change the world but I don't know what to do." That really is a great question: what should you do to make beneficial changes in the world? The answer is that you must change yourself. You must change not only what you do and say, but also what you hold to be true deep in your subconscious.

But how can you know what is truly in your subconscious mind? If you discover what is in your deep, true heart of hearts, how can you change what you find if you don't like it? Self-deception is the cause of much disappointment, so if you try to change yourself, how do you know the change is really made?

The answer to these questions lies in the process discussed in Chapter Sixteen. Only when you close your eyes, block out your conscious mind, and make the journey into your subconscious can you know what you truly believe about yourself and what you expect from life. Within the subconscious lies the knowledge of where you are now and where you want to go. Once you understand who you are and what you want, you can use the process of creativity for self-improvement and make the changes within yourself that are needed to achieve your goals.

When you have begun the process of self-improvement, you can relax and let other people do the same. The world will only change for the better when enough people have made changes within themselves by visualizing the requirements for their personal goals. As each individual person begins to actualize their vision of self-improvement, a natural evolution will occur and the entire world will change for the better. Law I, the Law of Consciousness, requires that this be so.

CHAPTER FOURTEEN

Evil Actions

*S*everal friends who have previewed the early manuscript of this book have asked, what if this information falls into the wrong hands? Can this process be used to do negative, destructive things? Unfortunately, the answer is yes. We know that ignorant, violent, self-absorbed people exist; the media bombards us with their deeds every day. There is no doubt that there are people with little consciousness development who can, and do, either knowingly or unknowingly, cause evil to happen. Laws I and II ultimately address these concerns in the following way.

To begin with, good and evil are the extremes of the concept encompassing our expectations of human behavior. At our level of existence, good and evil provide boundaries for our actions. Persons who become aware of the process for creation will understand there are repercussions from consciously creating evil and will avoid doing it at all costs.

Once you begin to use the creative process, believe me, you step into a different league where the rewards are great but the punishment for misuse is harsh. If you intend to use the creative process for evil purposes, put this book down now and read no further. The price you will pay for consciously misusing the process will be devastating. The worst part will be the knowledge that what you receive from the distorted use of the intended direction of the power to create will be what you created for your self. Trust me, do not think you can fool around with the power to create and use it for your own gain without repercussions. Use your gift well or not at all.

The other guard against evil actions is found within your own consciousness. As you become more proficient at using the creative process you will become acutely aware that your life is constructed by your thoughts. Understanding this will enable you to avoid personal experience with negative, hurtful situations even though they exist. You can prevent the pain and negativism that exists in the world from entering into your own life if you do not dwell on the negative side of life but instead direct your thoughts to accomplishment of your goals.

Personally, I work very hard on this aspect of my life. I don't go to horror movies or watch violence on television because they open me up to the violence they portray. For this reason, I don't watch the news before going to bed. I don't want the impressions of murderers, thieves and horrific accidents creating visions in my subconscious while I sleep.

The ability to protect your consciousness against the negativity and evil that exists in the world is a key element for the creation of happy, successful life. It is just as important as learning to direct and control your thoughts and visualize your goals.

CHAPTER FIFTEEN

Visualizing a Successful Life

Your mind has the power to create your material and spiritual life from the peanut butter of the universe. Since visualization is the process of creating mental pictures, the ability to visualize lies at the heart of the creative process. You can create a successful life by using the knowledge of whom you are and what you think you deserve as the guidelines for what you create.

Discovering what you want and creating an exact vision of what you desire is the keystone of success. This is a most important point, and one that needs to be repeated over and over again: *if you are to create something out of the peanut butter of the universe, you must learn to repeatedly create specific, clear, consistent mental pictures* of what you want. Clarity and specificity are vital to creating a successful life.

Developing the ability of creative visualization requires several steps. These steps are specific and necessary to ensure that the pictures we envision represent exactly what we want. In the 1960s, a common saying that moved through society was, "Be careful what you wish for, because you might get it." The process that will be presented next is the method of getting what you wish for, and making sure that what you wish for is exactly what you want.

The process has several steps. The first one is learning to relax.

Relaxation: Relaxation is an inwardly focused state of awareness in which the everyday cares and concerns of life, both mental and physical, are released from consciousness. Relaxation is not solely a physical state; lying in a hammock by a beach will not necessarily relax you. To relax, you must allow your consciousness to set aside your cares and replace them with a sense of calm and peacefulness. A relaxed person creates a mental state where the conscious brain is put on hold so that the subconscious mind can remove the barriers to achievement such as worry and stress, and allow the natural creative energy forces that are within your body to work freely.

Peaceful Scene: To achieve relaxation, it is helpful to visualize a scene. Typically, it is a peaceful scene in nature, one in which you feel relaxed. Some people naturally prefer a tropical setting with a beach and palm trees. Others may prefer the mountains with a cool waterfall and shady, massive trees. Still others prefer a foggy seashore with the sounds of waves crashing, or a hammock under a shade tree in a quiet neighborhood. The relaxing scene does not have to be outdoors. It could be a cozy room with a fireplace or your favorite chair in a sunny kitchen. Anyplace you can imagine that relaxes you will work fine.

You may not be able to think of a place that you are sure will relax you right now, but be assured one will present itself in your mind when you are ready. You will probably visualize the same scene each time you visit your relaxing scene. But it's fine if after a span of time your subconscious mind creates a different place to relax. My relaxing scene in nature has changed four or five times in the past 25 years and will most likely change again. All that's important is that you have a picture in your mind of a place where you can go to relax. If it changes, don't fight the change. Just go along with it and enjoy your new place to relax.

A common issue arising out of initial attempts at visualization is whether the relaxing scene you picture will really work for you. The point here is to understand that you cannot intellectualize relaxation. By intellectualizing, I mean trying to figure out beforehand, using your mind at the objective level to figure out, what you "should" experience at the subjective level.

Intellectualizing, especially for logic and math-oriented people, can be a problem when first learning to use the subconscious mind. Many "left brained" people see a problem and immediately attempt to arrive at a logical solution rather than letting their subconscious and their "right" brain be a part of their decision making process too. However, once the "left brain" people learn to use both the logical and subjective, creative parts of their brain, they benefit greatly from the combination; the point is to trust your subconscious mind and to use it all. So, if your peaceful scene relaxes you, it's the right one. Don't worry about how you think your relaxing scene will look to others; no one is ever going to see it but you.

Your creative consciousness is set up to provide only the functional solutions that work personally for you. Your creative consciousness concerns itself with taking the most effective course of action for you alone. It does not take into account current social trends or expectations you think that other people will have of you. Remember, your life is not a test and you will not be graded on the visions in your mind or how you choose to relax. The only aspect of your subconscious effort that people will ever be able to see is the result of what you do in the objective world. Rest assured that if you can relax in the place you have created, it is the right place.

54

To get into the correct mental state for relaxation and creation, it is best to go through a definite process each time. The process requires a sense of non-striving, by which I mean that you should not consciously work at getting what you want. Do not consciously try to direct your thoughts to a place where you, at the objective level, think you "should" be. Let your subconscious mind take control and direct itself to a vision it wants to reveal to you. As you continue into the investigation of your mind, you may be amazed to find there is a vast difference between who you objectively think you should be and what you subconsciously believe you are. We will discuss the differences between the two parts of ourselves later. For now, let your inner self take control.

The following steps will guide you to a mental state where you can create a relaxing scene in nature. When you are in your relaxing scene, your brain will slow its conscious activity so the subconscious can come to the fore and begin the process of creating your future.

Begin by reading the steps completely through several times until you understand what to do. Be assured that being in your relaxing scene or any deeper state of mind will not prevent you from responding to events at the objective level. You will be able to hear the telephone ring or respond to a family member's call or anything else that needs your immediate attention. It is as if your objective mind is on hold, though still instantly available if you need it.

The more you practice entering your levels of mind, the quicker you can train your objective mind to let go and relax. The relaxation you will strive for is not only a physical relaxation but also a sense of peace and serenity. In this state of serene relaxation, you will, in time, begin to sense the perfection of the universe.

Breathing: One physical key to knowing you are relaxed is a slowing of the breathing process. A person in a relaxed state can substantially reduce their breaths per minute from their normal resting rate. You not only will take fewer breaths but also breaths that are gentler, shallower, and that require less effort.

Time: Do not concern yourself with the passage of time. What is important is that you stay in your scene until you relax. There is no time limit in achieving the state of relaxation. Most people, when they use the process of creative visualization, stay in their relaxing scene only a short time - several minutes or so - before moving deeper into their subjective mind. However, in your first attempts to reach the subjective mind, it is important to remain in your relaxing scene for as long as it takes you to recognize that you are, in fact, relaxed. The time does not matter as long as you recognize that this process does, in fact, relax you. After a little practice you will quickly become confident and comfortable with your ability to enter, relax and leave your peaceful scene.

Beginning the process of creating a relaxing scene requires only four steps. Remember, don't do this yet. Read the whole book first:

1. **Find a comfortable chair** away from distractions. Remove glasses, jewelry or any other objects that might distract your awareness from your task. Don't lie on a bed since your relaxed state may make you want to go to sleep and you do not want to sleep during this exercise.

2. **Gently close your eyes and breathe slowly and deeply.** I find I breathe best when I breathe in and out gently and fully through my nose. If you have a stuffy nose, don't worry about how you breathe, just do it as gently and fully as you can. After a few breaths, notice that the tension throughout your body is beginning to lessen. If you become aware of specific points of tension such as clenched fists, tight jaws or any other area of tension, (often in the

legs or stomach), direct your awareness to those areas and allow them to relax.

3. **Direct your awareness to the area on the inside of your forehead above your eyebrows.** You may have the impression that your eyes are also looking up there too. This area is called the screen of the mind. All your inner visions should be projected here. Once you have relaxed and directed your inner awareness to the screen of the mind, let your mind begin to create your relaxing scene.

4. **Do not let your objective mind resist what your subjective mind creates**. Even if you are a tough athlete and you create a baby crib where you can relax and suck your thumb, go right ahead. Your relaxing scene is a private matter. What do you care what it looks like so long as you relax?

Relax and enjoy your peaceful place. Get into it, and experience what you have created for yourself. Call all your five senses into play. Physically move your hands to touch things you see there. Laugh, cry, or smile with delight. While you are in your relaxing scene, if it is a sunny place, allow the sun to feel warm on your skin. If there are flowers there, move your hands, take them to your nose, smell them, and feel how soft and delicate they are. If you feel compelled to act like a kid again and take off your shoes and run through a meadow or skinny-dip in a tropical sea, go right ahead and do it. (Of course, you do this in your mind and don't leave your seat.) Your relaxing scene in nature is yours to enjoy. Besides, it is happening only in your mind, so let go and have fun.

Physical Involvement: The process of getting physically involved with your visualizations is important to the creation of your sense of relaxation because physical involvement, even though you are sitting and imagining the situation in your mind, serves as validation of your mental activity. Reaching out to touch and smell a flower that exists only in your mind makes the vision seem more real. Experience your peaceful scene in nature and generate a feeling of calm relaxation. You will know it is time to go when a quiet feeling of needing to move on comes over you. Don't resist the feeling: take a moment to compose yourself and leave. When you feel you are ready to leave, turn your back on your relaxing scene and take 12 steps away from it. At the end of the 12th step, open your eyes slowly and rejoin the objective world. You may need to read these directions several times before you get comfortable with them. It may help to have a friend read the directions and help you through them the first time or two.

By the way, becoming physically involved in your visualization efforts looks positively weird to those who don't understand what you are doing. Therefore it is best to get totally involved, with hands and gestures aiding your subjective mind, in private. That is not to say that you can't visit your peaceful scene in public. I do it all the time when I am on a plane, riding in a car or sitting in a waiting room. But in public places I keep my physical activity to a minimum.

The OK System: A mental device called the "OK system," can be used to help you remember these directions. The OK system goes like this: Sit in a comfortable chair, close your eyes as if you are entering your relaxing scene, and make an OK sign with your thumb and forefinger. Rest the OK sign on your lap or leg with your palm up. Then take several deep, relaxing breaths and, once your mind is clear and calm, tell yourself that whenever you make an OK sign, whatever you hear, read or see will be remembered and recalled to a much higher degree than you have ever been capable of before. Your brain already records all the events that you have ever experienced; recalling them is the only problem. The OK system will help you do this, as it is an effective method of dramatically improving your ability to recall all events stored in your memory. If you use the OK system, you will be amazed at how well it works. Try it and see for yourself. Test the OK system out right now. Relax and make an OK sign and read the instructions for going into your relaxing scene again. Then close your eyes, create a mental picture of what they are and review them in your mind. Then open your eyes and check to see how well it worked. Remember; don't actually go into your peaceful scene now. Just use the OK system to memorize the four points.

I use the OK system all the time, especially when I know that what I am hearing of seeing is worth remembering, like in a class or when I want to remember directions. I remember using the OK system to memorize the VIN number on my car. I read the number, closed my eyes, and visualized the number on the screen of the mind (the place in the inside of your head, above your eyes) a few times, and there it was.

I've got my wife fooled into thinking I'm smart because I can recall the events of my life very well. She was astounded the other day when I recalled the capital of Paraguay with apparent ease. I'm not particularly intelligent, but it may seem that way because I use the OK system to input information and can, therefore, recall it easily. If you practice the use of the OK system in a class you will be amazed at how much more you can recall when test time rolls around.

Some people, because of prior mental programs, have real trouble with their relaxing scene in nature and using the OK system. They feel silly and self-conscious enjoying themselves in such a fun and frivolous way. They think that memorization takes a lot of hard work. If you find yourself in this category, don't worry. Your subconscious self has a true need to relax so it can function efficiently and your difficulty with letting go and relaxing will fade and disappear if you keep trying.

The OK system will work for you too. It's just that you'll have to give up a program called "I don't have a photographic memory," and an attachment, "I have to struggle and work hard if I want to get ahead." Once you release the objective level working of your mind and let the subjective level take over, it will happen. If you are one of these types of people, letting go of the objective mind and allowing the subjective mind to drive your life can be difficult, especially if you have had no experience with doing it. But once you try it, you will see for yourself how easy it is. So give it a shot. What do you have to lose?

The reason many people don't or can't relax is because they worry too much about how they look or what other people think of them. In my job as a middle school teacher, I see these aspects of adolescent behavior all the time. The self-centered concerns are understandable in young teens as they develop their identity. However, the "how do I look to others" and "what will people think" programs need to be set aside as you mature. If you are one of the many adults still being controlled by programs generated in your adolescence, you may want to examine them to see if they still work for you. The way to effectively examine them is coming up in Chapter Twenty-One.

As you begin this first phase of developing your process of creation, you may want to go into your peaceful, relaxing scene in a place where you are sure you will not be interrupted. This will help you to not feel so self-conscious about doing the work of relaxation. Make no mistake though, you must learn to set the cares of the world aside for a time and completely relax if you wish to create your life through creative visualization. There will be no point in continuing with the rest of the creative process until you can master this step.

Advancing to the next step in the creative process assumes that you can achieve a relaxed state of mind. Therefore, it is essential that you be able to relax in your relaxing scene. If you skip the relaxing step, you may run into difficulties later with your creation process because you might begin the creative process in an agitated state of mind. An agitated state of mind may often produce internal tension that may block you from understanding the true state of your inner feelings and expectations. You could not be certain that your subjective impressions truly represent where you stand. It is essential to know at what point you need to start your creative projects.

In addition, relaxation is essential because unless you can determine your true feelings about the issue you are dealing with in your subjective level of mind, you won't know how to proceed. You want to be sure that what you wish for is truly what is best for you. Only in a relaxed state of mind can you really trust your feelings. Take as much time as you need to practice relaxing before you continue. You should be able to slip easily and comfortably into and out of your relaxing scene in nature before going deeper into the process.

While we are on the subject of a proper creative frame of mind, I need to remind you that any medicines, chemicals or substances that create an altered state of mind should be avoided during the creative process. If you truly want to create a better life, you must be sure that you are clearheaded. You do not have to give up medicines you need or diversions you enjoy to have a successful life. But you must not use substances that will cloud your true feelings during the creative process. If you do use them, you must let their effects wear off and be completely free of their influence while you are in your levels of mind creating your life. If you are dependent upon such substances, use the creative process to end your dependency. A discussion of how to do this is presented in Chapter Thirty-Three. Once you have accomplished this task you can begin to create a better life for yourself.

CHAPTER SIXTEEN

Meditation

*W*hat you have been learning when acquiring the skills needed to relax is basic form of meditation. I have avoided that term until now so you could understand it for yourself before knowing its name. Meditation carries a lot of unnecessary, and sometimes negative, baggage in our western European oriented culture. This is unfortunate because nothing is more beneficial for your total health than meditation. Meditation is nothing new and it is the only gateway to effective application of the universal laws.

The western world often associates meditation with eastern religions and philosophies. While it is true that many religions in Asia practice meditation, it is not necessary that you take on their culture, religion or styles of dress to participate in meditation. Meditation does not require any stylized poses like those you see in TV commercials. You don't need a silk cushion, baggy pants, a turban or any other prop to go into your levels of mind. On the other hand, while it is not necessary to adopt the rituals of another culture to meditate, you can if you wish to. Either way it makes absolutely no difference.

It is important to note that meditation does not require a philosophy or a religion to be valid. I am an ordinary man and a Christian; I meditate effectively in jeans and a tee shirt in my office chair. The point of meditation is to create a pathway to your subconscious mind through relaxation and not the promotion of any particular religion.

They're many benefits that result from relaxation by meditation. The most important is that when a person relaxes they reduce stress and become calmer, happier and can function more effectively. Any athlete can attest to benefit of relaxation in sports performance. The great athletes of the world amaze us with their skills. They do not consciously try to perform well; in fact they do the opposite. They go into the "zone," a mental place where they are alert and completely relaxed with all their skills the have practiced for so long, immediately available to them. They let what they have practiced flow naturally out of them without conscious effort.

Relaxation is the most obvious benefit of the meditative process, but there are many more. To achieve other benefits it will be necessary to go deeper into your levels of mind. Once again, it should be noted that you would always be able to emerge from your levels of mind, no matter how deep you go, instantly and with no ill effects, if the need should arise. The reason to meditate in the deep levels of mind is to make sure that you leave your objective mind out of your dealings with your subconscious mind. Remember, it is in your deep subconscious mind that the ideas and programs with which you create your present life are kept.

CHAPTER SEVENTEEN

The Structured Process

*T*he functions of the mind, both its conscious and subconscious parts, are interwoven into a highly complex system. The complexity of the interactions of the various aspects of the mind creates a clutter of information that makes it a difficult place in which to work. In order to deal with the complexity of the mind you need to have a process of entering, working within and leaving the mind that bypasses the mind's clutter and complexity.

If you simply close your eyes and seek to communicate with the subconscious without creating a structured system, everything you experience there will seem vague, unordered and disconnected. The structured process allows you to create a path to access the information and abilities stored within you without getting lost or stuck in the maze of possibilities that whir around in your mind. Think of it like a system of ropes used to enter and leave a dark cave. Without a system to work in the mind, you will see, for the most part, unclear shapes and shifting forms of gray, red and black. These vague and shifting forms will represent visions and programs you have stored within you.

The framework for the process is like training wheels on a bicycle. For the most adept humans, those few who are experienced at voyaging into their mind, a structured process is not necessary. But for the average person, like you and me, the process is essential because it speeds up the time it takes to create clear, repeatable visions. Moreover, a lack of structure will provide no starting or stopping point for your future creative sessions. And a clear, repeatable vision of your goals is required for directed imagery creation. So, in order to create clear, repeatable visions of the goals you want to reach, you will need to create a structured format that I call a workshop and assistants.

The workshop and assistants will provide the structure you need to accomplish your goals. In the workshop, you will create tools, and methods to help you work within yourself. You will also create personal assistants that you can rely on for guidance. Your assistants will exist only in your workshop but they will become, over time, the most real and valuable friends you will ever have. Many young children create imaginary friends for companionship; that's the sort of thing you are going to do.

The structure of the workshop will help you use the powers locked within your subjective self. Your assistants will help you make the decisions that will direct you to your goals. Within the workshop, with the aid of your assistants, you will be able to decide what you want for yourself. You will decide how you really feel about what you think you want, whether or not you think you deserve it, and what steps you need to take to make it manifest in your life.

Once you have started the process of creation, you can review your progress and decide on your next step. Once you begin the process of creation, you can relax, let go and not worry while the process is taking place. After some practice and some small-scale successes, you will know for certain that what you create in your workshop will come into existence in your everyday life.

CHAPTER EIGHTEEN

The Vacation Home

*B*efore you go further into the creative process, you should practice what you have learned to sharpen your visualization skill. What you are going to do next is go to your relaxing scene and build a small vacation home. Please read all the directions before starting. Use the OK technique to help you with the directions. Remember, don't do this now, but wait until you have read the entire book.

Go to a quiet place and enter your relaxing scene. Spend a minute or two relaxing and getting comfortable. Then look around your scene and find a place to build a small vacation house. When finding a place to build the house, do not be limited in any way by the location or condition of your relaxing scene. If your relaxing scene is in the middle of the ocean, you may have to build a boathouse, a raft, a submarine or whatever you decide. You are going to be practicing your creative visualization techniques at the subjective level and you should not be concerned with any "practical" barriers you have created at the objective level.

When you build your house, use your hands in the process just as you actually would even though your eyes are closed. Physical activity is important to creative visualization because it activates more parts of the mind. The increased mental activity will have the effect of making the vision seem more real. This sense of reality will create strong and vivid images that you will be able to recall and reproduce. Also, images that are strong and clear will be more acceptable to your subconscious. The secret to a successful, fulfilling, life is to create over and over again strong, clear visions of what you want. Vague dreams and desires are good starting places, but bright, clear images are best for creation.

Building a house in your mind is fun and easy to do even if you're not a carpenter. You may not realize it yet, but you already know how. All that is required is to do what seems necessary. Clear the lot, build a level foundation, make a frame for the walls, floor and roof, put in the pipes and electricity, put on the roof, cover the walls, apply a little paint if you feel you need it, and you're done. If you are one of those people who are really "carpentry challenged" and have no faith in your building skills, just create several highly skilled carpenters in your relaxing scene to help you. If you need them, they will be there; look around your relaxing scene until you find them. When you see them, ask them over. They will be glad to help. Tell them what you want to build, and they will do the rest.

The point of the exercise is to experience the ease and fun of creative visualization and not worry about your lack of skill. Remember, all original creative work begins with an idea that usually does not have much supporting experience. If we did have experience with our creations, they wouldn't truly be creations but be recollections or different applications of what we already know. The subconscious mind will tap into the universal mind for information that you need to complete your vacation house whenever you need it. You will create the carpenters as a plausible outlet for the information you receive from the universal mind on how to build a house. So, even though you can't hang a picture, go right ahead and build your vacation house. You can do it. Your subconscious will show you how.

While in your relaxing scene, take time to enjoy your vacation house. Sit on the porch if there is one. Relax in the kitchen, open the refrigerator, look inside, and see if there is a cold soda or beer. If there is, take it out and enjoy it. Maybe back in the corner of the refrigerator is your favorite snack. What is it? Is it cold chicken, apple pie or a roast beef sandwich? Take out whatever it is and enjoy it. Do you want the whole pie? Go ahead and eat it all. Eat everything in the refrigerator; no one will know. Our subconscious has the capacity to do many important things for us. But the first and most important thing is for us to relax, have fun, and relieve the stress and tensions of the objective world.

Building your vacation home is an exercise in how to use your mind to tap into your creative powers. Include your vacation home as a part of your relaxing scene if you feel so inclined. If not, keep it as a separate place that's located between your relaxing scene in nature and the workshop we are going to build. You should not use your relaxing scene or your vacation home to do creative work because relaxing is a very important element of life and you need to save your relaxing scene strictly for relaxing. Let it be a mental playground where you can retreat and enjoy all the fun activities you can imagine.

The serious work of creating your successful life needs it's own special place in your mind. A place set aside only for goal setting, goal achievement visualization and other important tasks. The workshop you are going to build and the set of tools you will need to do the work you are going to do will be created next. It will be your special place to do the work of bringing your dreams and desires for your successful life into the objective, everyday world.

CHAPTER NINETEEN

The Colors of the Rainbow

O ne of the most important tools in your workshop is the colors of the rainbow. The colors represent mental states of mind that are essential to
understand when creating your new life. Reviewing your
colors as you enter your levels of mind helps you to know
when you feel emotionally or physically upset, lack courage or a sense of inner peace.

Creating your future when you are agitated is not recommended because projects begun in an agitated state will
have to be abandoned. They will lack a stable, emotional
foundation needed for creating what you truly want. This
so because once your emotions calm down what you want
may change too. If, as you begin your entry into your subconscious, you become aware of emotional or physical imbalances, it is better to deal with them at that point rather
than starting to create something that will have to be abandoned later. Only if you have yourself in a relaxed and peaceful
frame of mind should you begin your creative visualizations.

Begin the process as you did when you created the relaxing scene in nature. Sit in a quiet place in a comfortable
sitting position and remove any physical distractions such
as glasses, contacts, tight belts, etc. Next, visualize the colors of the rainbow in the order described on the following

pages. Take moment in your relaxing scene to prepare your mind to enter your deeper subconscious.

When beginning this exercise you will run down the colors as a way to enter your meditation **before** you briefly visit your relaxing scene. As with all subjective things, the thought of the color is what is important, not the actual color. For example, while trying to visualize the color red, you may not actually be able to visualize it. It is sufficient if you can visualize an object that you know is red, like a ripe tomato. Don't waste time by spending a half-hour trying to bring the exact color to mind. The point of reviewing colors is to become aware of how you feel about yourself before you begin the work of creation.

For color references, I use familiar objects like fruit, cars or natural objects like the sky, trees or water. As you review your colors, be aware of whether or not you have difficulty visualizing a certain color. Difficulty visualizing a certain color will give you a key about your personal inner state. If you have trouble visualilzing something purple, for example, you may have trouble identifying your life's purpose. If this is the case, you should spend time in your levels determining what your purpose in life is and save your creative efforts for another day.

Color review is essential to creation; never enter or leave your levels without reviewing them. The colors you must bring to mind and the order of visualization are as follows:

RED. Red is associated with physical things, energy, strength and vitality. If you are physically weak and lacking vitality in life, shine a red light on yourself.

ORANGE. Orange is associated with emotions. If your emotions are not under control, you may need to shine an orange light on yourself or work to calm your emotions before continuing the creative process.

YELLOW. Yellow is the color associated with the intellect and intellectual processes. You would shine a yellow light on yourself as you prepare for a test or presentation.

GREEN. Green is the color associated with peace, calmness and healing. If you feel the absence of peace and calm, shining a green light on yourself will calm and relax you. If you are ill, green light will enable you to heal yourself.

BLUE. Blue is the color of love. Love in this context refers to the warm acceptance and caring feeling towards others. If you want to project your loving feelings towards someone, or make your home a loving place shine a blue light on them.

PURPLE. Purple is the color associated with your life goals and personal destiny. If you want to get in touch with the personal core of yourself or your personal destiny, shine a purple light on yourself.

VIOLET. Violet is the color associated with your personal spirit or soul. Violet represents the deep motivation and spiritual origin of your actions.

Review the colors as you enter and leave your levels of mind. If you note imbalances in how you react to your colors, shine a light, paint yourself, wrap a cloth or put on a shirt of the color you need as you leave your levels. You can mix two colors together if you feel the need to do two things. However, if you are upset for several reasons, the best thing to do is shine a brilliant white light on yourself. White light is not part of the color review process prior to going to your workshop level. But because white light is the result of the mixture of all light frequencies, a white light can be used as a general cleansing method. A white light will be installed over the door to your workshop and can be used as you enter and leave your workshop. This is done to ensure that if you must deal with difficult tasks in your workshop such as death, divorce or crimes you previously committed, t you can cleanse yourself of the negativity surrounding these events and not transport the negativity back with you to the objective level.

As you gain experience with the process of color review, you will be delighted at how effective you are at establishing and maintaining a sense of inner peace. This is so because it is in the subjective mind that we are most clearly connected to the universal mind, and it is in the universal mind that the energy needed for the specific benefit that each color provides is generated.

The colors can be projected anytime, whether you are in the objective or subjective level of mind. Whenever I see an ambulance or fire truck go by, I always project a white light on it to assist accomplishment of the perfect end result, whatever that is supposed to be. Colors can be of great value to us as we go through the day. What you must do now is create a workshop where you can use your colors and the creative process to create your life as you wish it to be.

If you read further into the subject of metaphysics, as some of you might, you will find that different authors, with different backgrounds and different cultures, use colors different from the ones I have presented to represent the range of human emotions. The amazing thing is that all the colors work if the users of the colors believe they will (Remember, Law I is always at work). For example, let's say you read somewhere that pink represented the emotion of love rather than blue. And, as a result of your reading, you used the color pink in your levels of mind to broadcast your feelings of love instead of blue. Your feelings of love for people and situations would be cast into the universal mind, and the persons or situations would greatly benefit by your projections of love with the same effect as the color blue. Daniel Webster once said, "Thought is the process by which human ends are ultimately answered." The importance of the color lies in the belief you attach to it. This is consistent with Law I. So, if you think blue represents love it does but if you think pink represents love it does too.

When you want to project your loving thoughts you can; the color you use is only the vehicle of the emotion. I have used the colors of the rainbow to represent human emotion for several good reasons. First, they are colors of nature contained in pure light and are revealed to us in rainbows and refracted light from prisms. Second, they were the colors I was taught to use. And third, I know they work.

CHAPTER TWENTY

Creating Your Workshop

*T*he workshop is a place you create in your subconscious mind in which to plan your life's work.
The design and appearance of the workshop are
completely up to you. When constructing a workshop remember that there is no right or wrong way to do it. When
you create your workshop in your mind, no matter how it
looks, it will serve the creative purpose perfectly.

I have provided a diagram with some tools for you to
use in your workshop. It is important that all the tools in
the diagram are in your workshop, but it is not necessary
that they be in the exact place that I put them. The diagram
I have provided has walls, but it's not required that the
workshop have walls. What is necessary is that all the equipment and tools in the diagram be in your workshop and
arranged so that you can readily use them.

There is no place that is best to have a workshop. Yours
can be a castle made of clouds, a cavern made of solid gran-
ite, or a glass bubble under the sea. Whatever you imagine
will be perfect. Your workshop represents one aspect of your
inner vision of yourself; examine it carefully when you are
done.

Creating a workshop requires that we go to a deeper
level of the subconscious mind than we did for our relaxing
scene in nature. Therefore, the process is modified to allow

for the need to go deeper into your subconscious. Before we begin, remember that it is necessary to **read the directions completely through several times** (using the OK system) until you are confident that you understand what to do before you attempt to do it.

In the workshop, all the tools, equipment, reference manuals and physical workspace necessary to complete any project that you can imagine will be present. In the following diagram, (Fig.1) a location for each item in your workshop is carefully laid out. The location of each item is not as important as the subjective realization that anything you need to complete your projects is readily available. Since most people know very little about the things they want to create, your assistants will be created to offer you guidance. We will create our assistants later. For now, please use the diagram in the initial stages of your creative efforts. This will ensure that your subconscious knows that all the tools it needs are in place.

Creating a workshop is an essential portion of the creative process. Therefore, it is recommended that an hour or so be set aside where you can devote all your efforts to this task. Creating the workshop is easy, but there are many pieces to this part of the puzzle. So, it's is strongly advised that you read all the way to the end of the chapter in one sitting. Also, do not try to build a workshop until you have reviewed the workshop diagram and read all the parts and requirements of the task. You will want to have a mental picture of the entire process before you begin any part of it.

It will be helpful to have a friend read the location of the equipment in the workshop to you while you are in your levels. Having a friend help you is good but not necessary, as you can use the OK system to remember where to position the equipment. You can also "cheat" in your levels by having the diagram close at hand and open your eyes to

WORKSHOP

FIG. 1

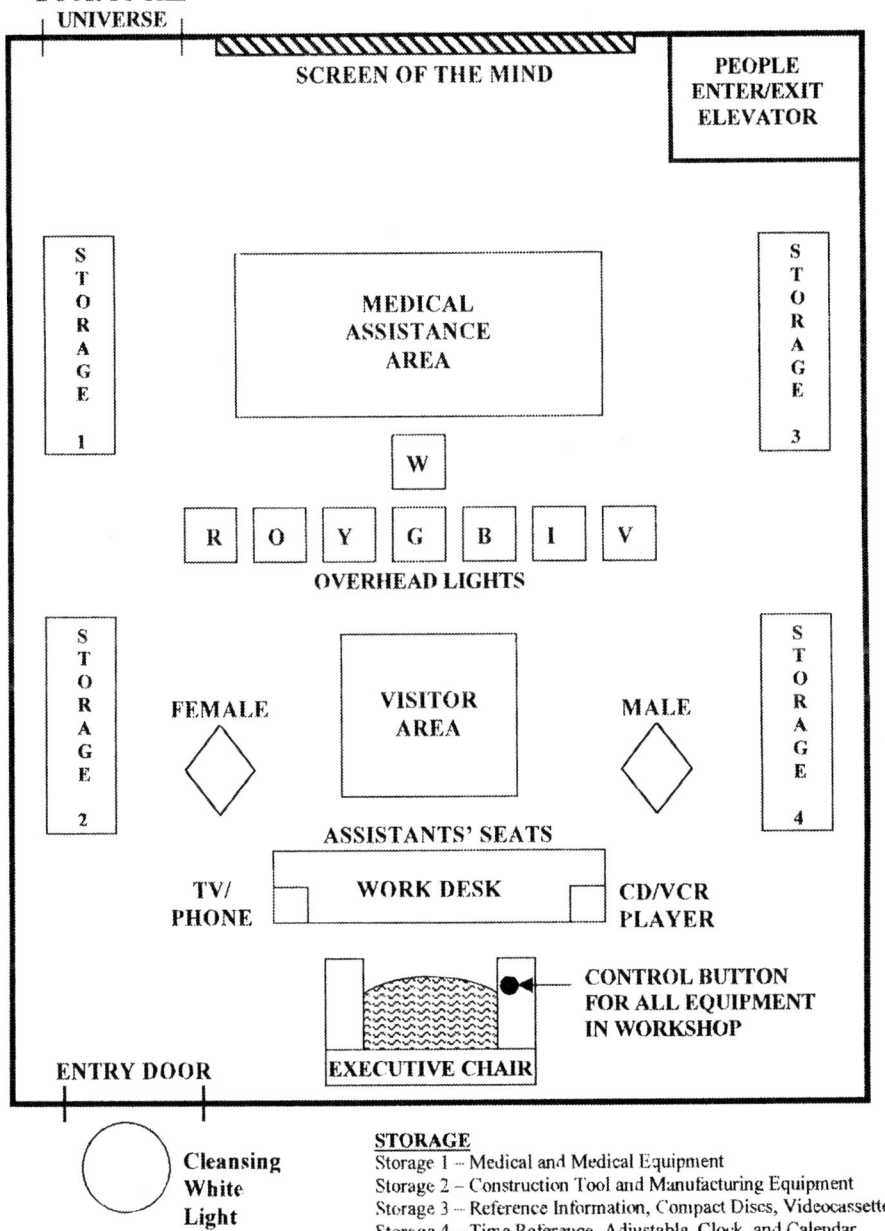

DOOR TO THE UNIVERSE

SCREEN OF THE MIND

PEOPLE ENTER/EXIT ELEVATOR

STORAGE 1

MEDICAL ASSISTANCE AREA

STORAGE 3

W

R O Y G B I V

OVERHEAD LIGHTS

STORAGE 2

FEMALE

VISITOR AREA

MALE

STORAGE 4

ASSISTANTS' SEATS

TV/ PHONE

WORK DESK

CD/VCR PLAYER

CONTROL BUTTON FOR ALL EQUIPMENT IN WORKSHOP

ENTRY DOOR

EXECUTIVE CHAIR

Cleansing White Light

STORAGE
Storage 1 – Medical and Medical Equipment
Storage 2 – Construction Tool and Manufacturing Equipment
Storage 3 – Reference Information, Compact Discs, Videocassette
Storage 4 – Time Reference, Adjustable, Clock and Calendar

take a quick peek. You can compose yourself easily and re-enter your meditative state once you have assured yourself of the location of the equipment.

Please do not become overly concerned as to whether or not you have gotten everything "right." If you miss something the first time, you can add it later. The important idea to get across is that all the tools and equipment you will ever need to complete your projects in the workshop are available to you. The diagram is provided so you can develop a mental picture of one example of how to organize your workshop.

Establishing a workshop is just like creating your small vacation house. The only difference is that the workshop exists as a tool to access the deep subconscious, and is a place where you go to do serious life planning and creation. It is not necessary that you have your workshop laid out exactly like the diagram. The essential element is the understanding that *everything* you need to create your life is available to you in your workshop. If you need to fly an airplane, don't worry if you don't know how to fly in the objective world. You can do anything in your workshop.

Creating a Workshop: Create a workshop requires the same process as building your vacation home. Sit in a quiet place, remove as many objective distractions as possible, close your eyes and relax. Take a few deep breaths and review your colors, continuing down the colors until you reach violet. Once you reach violet, you will see a way to drop further into your subconscious mind. It will appear before you as a door, a ladder, a slide or some means that will take you deeper into your mind. Take the passage 12 steps, or 12 rungs of a ladder down to your peaceful, relaxing scene. You will want to have the feeling that you are going deeper within yourself. When you arrive in your relaxing scene, pause for a moment to look around, take a few gentle, deep breaths and relax. Tell yourself that it is now time to create a workshop.

Spend only a moment relaxing in your scene, and then direct your awareness to the area behind your forehead and focus your attention there. As you focus your attention on, the screen of the mind, the area above your eyes and behind your forehead, a vision of the structure or place you will know to be your workshop will begin to develop. Do not tell yourself what the workshop will look like beforehand; let the subjective image come to you. Once a vision has been established, build your workshop as you did your vacation house, using carpenter helpers if you need them. Be sure to get your hands physically involved in the creative process. When you have finished step back and enjoy the beauty of your creation.

Workshops are as diverse as humanity; they can be a cabin in the woods, an executive suite in a modern office building, a floating bubble in the clouds or a cave under the ocean. All workshops are perfect for the owner. Do not concern yourself with the clarity of the mental image that you develop of your workshop. At times, the workshop will appear to be a vision of remarkable clarity; other times it can appear as vague images in red and black or shades of gray. In either instance, the workshop that you bring to mind will serve the processes of creation perfectly.

On the front of your workshop, notice a main entry door. Above the door, place a large lamp with a bright, white light in it. Enter your workshop by that door. The workshop may be empty or it may already have the equipment in place. Either way is fine. If there are people in your workshop, walk up close to them and quietly ask them to leave.

What is needed now is to place the equipment in your workshop if it is not already there or to review the equipment you have if it is already there. It is advisable at this point to have the diagram close at hand or a friend to read to you. Remember, the placement of the tools and equipment in the workshop is not required to be exactly like the diagram. The diagram is just one example of how to organize the equipment. When designing your executive chair, make sure that you have included all the control buttons and communication devices on the arms of the chair. You should not need to move around your workshop to do your work unless you want to.

Once the workshop is complete, sit in your executive chair and relax. Take as much time as you need to place the equipment in your workshop. Make sure that you like the style and look of the workshop, as it is a true reflection of your inner self. Use the control buttons to work the elevator doors. The doors must slide down from the top to open and rise up from the floor to close, (unlike a regular elevator that opens and closes from the sides). Make sure you locate the switch to turn on your colored lights one at a time. Use specific colors to work on specific areas. Use the white light as an overall cleansing and mood-boosting tool. Walk around your workshop; visit all the tools and materials locations. Be sure to notice the door to the universe in the back left of your workshop.

If you like, open the door and see the universe spread out before you. From this door, you can travel to anywhere you can imagine: any place on earth, any planet, star or galaxy. If for any reason you need to communicate with any spiritual beings or beings that have died, you can open this door, envision their names, and they will come to you and communicate with you in some fashion. They may not always use words but you will understand them perfectly. If a person in your life has died leaving unresolved issues between the two of you, this is an effective way to work them out and bring closure to an issue that is troubling to you.

Now that you have created your workshop, take a moment to admire your work. Walk around all parts of your new workshop and notice the perfection of your creation. Once you have familiarized yourself with your workshop, leave by the entry door. Once outside your workshop walk to your relaxing scene. But you will not need to stop there now. Locate the door to the objective world and take the twelve steps up the ladder or passageway and open the door to your colors. Review the colors briefly in reverse order: violet, purple, blue, green, yellow, orange and red. When you get to red, open your eyes and take a moment to adjust to the objective world. You will feel relaxed, refreshed and energized by your visit to your workshop.

Be advised, the look of your workshop will change over time as you change. This will reflect the changes that occur within you as your life progresses. No matter what your workshop looks like, the purpose of the workshop will always be the same and the tools in the workshop will always be available. As with all things subjective, do not resist the changes that will occur as your self-image changes over time. If you resist the new vision of your inner self, nothing bad will happen to you. It will just take longer for you to realize your goals. Take a day off before creating the final and most important element in your workshop.

CHAPTER TWENTY-ONE

Creating Your Assistants

Your personal assistants are merely subjective representations of the two major divisions within your subconscious mind: your passive/feeling nature and your active/aggressive nature. The purpose of the assistants is to provide a conduit for information stored in the universal mind needed to actualize your goals. Assistants also provide counseling and can be a sounding board for ideas and feedback on your progress as you create your successful life.

Your assistants work on the principle that two, or three, heads are better than one. The assistants act as guidance counselors through their actions, words and expressions. Your assistants have the capacity to review your actions in the objective world and offer suggestions or advice in a private, nonjudgmental setting. Since the assistants are aspects of your own subconscious, they are always on your side and act in loyal support of your best interests. However, they do not always agree with the actions directed by your conscious mind in the objective world. They may act in surprising ways or express points of view you would not normally attribute to the image you have of them. They will be the first to let you know if you are not acting in your own best interest. In time, you will realize that your assistants have a limitless ability to be of service to you and will be your most trusted friends who will never let you down.

Your assistants, no matter who they appear to be, are aspects of you and not authority figures that try to control you or mold you to an ethical standard to which you do not already subscribe. They may look like people you already know or people you know about. Often they take the form of movie stars, athletes, or famous people you look up to. It is also possible that they will be people who you don't know at all. Either way is fine. Your assistants are visions that represent your conception of your active/aggressive nature or your passive/feeling nature. They are you, not the people you have heard about in the objective world.

When dealing with your assistants, bear in mind you are dealing with yourself. Since you and all others are unique, the advice and assistance they give you will be valid only for you. Do not take the advice your assistants give you and apply it to someone else. For example, do not tell a friend to give up candy because your assistants told you to give up candy. It is better that you follow your inner heart and allow your friend to do the same. If, from a place of sincere service to others, you sense an imbalance within another person that you feel would benefit by your assistance, there is a better way to be of service to them than to give them advice. We have discussed service in Chapter Thirteen and will discuss the topic further and in much more detail in Chapter Thirty. But first, you must learn to help yourself.

The passive/feeling side of your subjective nature is represented in the workshop by a female form. A male form represents your active/aggressive side. The divisions of the subconscious mind into the two parts are made so that you can develop an evenhanded approach to your life. Creating assistants to assume these dissimilar roles serves as a valuable internal balancing mechanism. The labels of female for passive/feeling and male for active/aggressive are not meant to imply that all females are passive or that all males are aggressive. Even the most cursory observation of human behavior will show that to be false and that all people have both characteristics.

The division of the subconscious in this way is a useful tool to gain a wider more balanced approach to life. If, for example, you are female and your female assistant is dominant in every discussion, you may want to actively solicit the opinion of your male assistant. In this way, your plans and personal opinions will take on a more balanced and comprehensive nature. You will always have the free will to accept or not accept the guidance of your assistants. But my experience has been that they are always right. But they cannot make you do anything you don't want to do in the objective world. They will become those nagging, little voices of reason that remind you of your goals just when you are about to do something you will end up regretting. They may also whisper advice and warnings to you that you will remind you of things you must do and of difficulties you should avoid. I have had my assistants as my constant companions for over 25 years, and I cannot recall even one instance when they ever steered me wrong and many, many instances where they have been helpful in guiding me through the day to day events of my life. I do admit, however, that I don't always follow their advice and, as a result, my progress towards my goals has been slowed.

Creating your assistants is easy. But, as before, read and understand all the instructions before you begin. To start, we must return to the workshop via the color review and relaxing scene. As you enter your workshop by the entry door, pause for a moment and shine the white light over the door down on you. The white light will act as a cleansing device that will remove any remaining tension and unpleasantness from you prior to entering your workshop. This final cleansing process should only take a moment.

When you enter your workshop, take your executive seat and look around your workshop. The large screen of the mind should be clearly visible on the opposite side of your workshop from you elevated slightly above eye level. The door to the universe will be located to the left of the screen of the mind, and the people entry/departure elevator will be located to the right. In front of the screen of the mind is the medical assistance area. And in front of that will be the visitor's area. Mounted overhead is your array of colored lights. On the far left are your medicines and medical equipment storage. On the near left are your construction tools and manufacturing equipment. On the far right are your reference materials, and on the near right are your adjustable clock and calendar. To your immediate front is your desk, and on each side and slightly behind are two empty chairs reserved for your new assistants.

Take a moment to make sure your workshop is in good operating order. Turn on the lights one by one. Turn on your television, make a call to a friend, and use the buttons on the arm of your chair to open and close the elevator door. Remember, the door goes down and up, not side-to-side. Once you are sure that all is ready, sit in your chair and write on your screen of the mind, "I am ready to receive my male assistant; please take your place in the elevator." When you feel that he has entered the elevator, then, using the control button on the arm of your chair, slowly lower the elevator door. Observe your male assistant as the lowering door reveals him. His hair and forehead are exposed first, then the eyes, nose and cheeks. Next, his jaw and mouth are revealed. You should now stop the door and take a moment to look at his entire face. This is the face of your active/aggressive nature. Continue lowering the door slowly revealing his entire body. Notice how he is dressed. Invite him into your workshop. Ask him to walk around and notice his posture, manner of walking and overall bearing. Go over to him and shake his hand or hug him. Accept the person that is revealed to you and do not be concerned if your male assistant does not appear to you to be an active/aggressive type.

Express your happiness at finally meeting him. Your male assistant will probably be very glad to meet you too. Take a moment to show him around your workshop. Then invite him to sit in the chair across from you on the right side of your work desk. Take a moment to reflect on the look and manner of your male assistant. This is a picture of your active/aggressive self. If there are aspects of your male assistant's nature that you wish weren't there, make a mental note to ask your assistants, both of them, what you should do within yourself to change them. When you make those changes, do not be surprised if your male assistant changes too.

Use the same process to create your female assistant. On the screen of the mind write, "I am ready to receive my female assistant; please take your place in the elevator." When you feel she has entered the elevator, use the control button on the arm of your chair and slowly lower the door. Take note of her hair and forehead, then eyes, nose, cheeks, jaw and mouth. Hold the elevator door for a moment and examine her entire face. This is the face of your passive/feeling nature. Continue to slowly lower the door and reveal the rest of her body. Invite her into your workshop. Go over to her and shake her hand or give her a hug. Express your happiness at finally meeting her. She will, no doubt, be very glad to finally meet you too. Take a moment to show her around your workshop. Ask them their names and introduce them to each other. Don't be surprised to find that they have already met.

Once they have had a moment to become acquainted and are seated, explain to them that you have begun the process of taking direct control over your life. Tell them you will need their assistance for the rest of your life in planning and creating your future. Request that they be present, in their chairs, ready to assist you, every time you enter your workshop. As you prepare to leave your workshop, shake their hands or give them a hug and say good-bye. Rise from your chair, turn left to the exit door and depart from your workshop.

As you pass through the door, pause briefly to allow the cleansing white light to shine on you. Move to your relaxing scene (there is no need to pause here), and find the ladder or passage way up to your colors. Ascend the 12 levels to your colors, visualize your colors briefly in reverse order: violet, purple, blue, green, yellow, orange, and red. When you get to red, open your eyes and realize that you are alert, energized and ready to function at the objective level. Be sure to take a minute before getting up to prepare yourself for the conscious level of life.

CHAPTER TWENTY-TWO

Words of Caution

*N*ow you have all the elements of your workshop in place. You can now use the workshop to create your life the way you want it to be. But before you proceed to the next step, a word of caution is necessary.

What you have done to this point is to create a place within your subjective mind where you can do the work of creating a successful life. You have created a place to relax, a place to work and assistants to help you plan your work. You have done this for your personal benefit, in a private, secure place. It is important to remember that at the objective level of life most people have not been acquainted with the processes that you have just learned. They will not understand or appreciate you telling them about your experiences, no matter how excited you may be.

It is a bad idea for you to try to convince someone else of the value of this process, especially someone you truly care about. Keeping the process to yourself can be difficult, but you must learn to do it. Believe me, it is best that you do not discuss, explain, or try to teach anyone else the process that you have learned.

Because the process is not widely used in the objective world, people without an understanding of what you are doing will accuse you of being insane, crazy, a witch or a weirdo. They will do this either openly or behind your back simply because they do not understand. Ignorance is not bliss, and most people who don't understand what you are doing will undermine your efforts with negativism or derision.

Overcoming the negative energy of your friends will create an unnecessary drain on your energy because you will either try to explain the process or try to defend it. At the beginning stage of awareness of the process, you will not be capable of doing either. Even experienced persons who are adept at applying this process cannot explain the process to those who are not ready to receive the explanation. As I stated at the beginning of the book, the only real proof of the validity of these concepts lies in the personal experience you have when you use them.

Therefore, I strongly recommend that you give yourself the time to incorporate these processes into your life and develop a degree of self-assurance before exposing yourself to the criticism of the people in your life who are ignorant of the process. The best course of action is to for you to learn the process so well that you become a better person. By doing this you will become an example to your friends and co-workers. They will see for themselves the changes in you and will want to know how you made those changes.

If you talk about the concepts that guide the universe with those who have not gone through the same experience you have, some of them will test you and place demands on you that you cannot fulfill. They might say something like, "If you have all these powers and can have anything you want, make yourself a new car. Right now!" They will expect the car to drop down from the heavens right in front of them. As we will learn, the creative force does not work that way. My advice is that you never talk about this process to anyone, ever, unless you are sure they also understand the process too.

As you go through your life, you will, by the power of Law I, the Law of Consciousness, attract like-minded people to you. Once you know they have the same set of values (they may or may not have read this book), then you can expose yourself and share your experiences if you want to. I can assure you though that the greatest living masters of the laws of the universe are unknown to the public. If you truly feel you must discuss this matter with others, then give them your copy of this book and talk to them after they have read it. Other than that, I recommend that you make no statement about what you have learned except by the example of your life.

Now that you have all the tools in place, you need to begin to use the tools to benefit yourself and others. In the next chapter, you will learn the formula for creation and how it applies to your life. As always, you will need to work if you are to succeed. But from now on, the work will be goal-specific, and the results will be more satisfying because you will know that they are a direct result of your own creative efforts.

CHAPTER TWENTY-THREE

Creating a Successful Life

C reativity is a natural process that all human beings use every day. The process of creativity is derived from universal law. In review, there are two universal laws. The universal laws are the basis for your existence and everything you possess. Law I, the Law of Consciousness, states that whatever you hold in consciousness as being truly real for you becomes real. Law II, the Law of Return, states that whatever you hold in consciousness, as being true and real for you **and others** is what **you** receive. These two laws allow for a limitless range of possibilities for humankind. The essence of the process of creativity is that thoughts become real things or real situations. That means that the thoughts you have in your subconscious either create or attract to you tangible objects in the objective world without fail.

As you gain proficiency in using the laws, your failure to use the powers in accordance with the laws, may cause harm or misfortune to others but will most certainly cause harm to you. This is especially true as you gain expertise in use of the powers. If, for example, a person with my experience at using the laws should knowingly steal even a penny, I should expect to lose everything I have. You might say that's not fair because I stole only a penny and lost so much more in return. But the law of returns does not understand or deal in dollar amounts. It deals in concepts. If I steal any-thing of any amount, then I am opening up myself to be stolen from in any amount.

So, be advised that personally beneficial creativity re-quires that it be exercised within the restraints of Law II. The everyday application of the laws is not really difficult if you follow the direction of your assistants because they will know the right course of action to take in any circum-stance. You have been warned twice against the misuse of the power of creativity.

The process of creation has already been presented to you in the process of visualization in your workshop. Hav-ing what you want is merely a process of entering your workshop and checking with your assistants to make sure that what you want is good for you, and then projecting a clear image of what you want on the screen of the mind. To have your image manifest in your objective life, the visual-ization process may have to be repeated many times. The time it takes to manifest an image depends upon the com-plexity of the thing you desire, how many other people are involved, and how many personal changes you need to un-dergo in order to feel that you deserve what you envision. But no matter how long it takes, what you feel you deserve will be created. The formula for creation never fails. The way to put this formula to personal use is now at hand.

The formula used to create all that is, all that has ever been, and all that will ever be is as follows:

IDEA/IMAGE + EMOTION + PERSONAL ACTION = MANIFESTATION

Idea/image means imagination and to imagine means to "image in" your mind. You cannot create something that you can't imagine or make an image of in your mind. Do not be confused by the fact that you may experience situations at the objective level of life that you didn't personally imagine in your subconscious mind. Remember, all people create. Their creations are in the world too and you may unwittingly become part of them. To understand this, a more complete discussion of involuntary involvement in negative events is required.

As we all know, the thought that only good things happen does not coincide with the reality of the world. There are people in the world, as any television newscast or newspaper will tell you, who think harmful, destructive thoughts and do terrible things. To think, or pretend to think otherwise is foolish. There are also people who feel that negative actions or accidents don't happen to good people by chance. They believe that everything is the result of the thoughts held in consciousnesses of all the people involved in any particular action. This position is, in my opinion, extreme because actions can happen to infants and young people who couldn't have possibly held negative thoughts about the events that harmed them; birth defects, car accidents, and the many forms of child abuse are examples.

I am not prepared to discuss this issue to a hard and fast conclusion because my understanding of the application of the laws is still far from clear on every point. I firmly believe that Law I applies without exception, but I also believe that a person can be in the wrong place at the wrong time and be involved in situations that are not of their own making. This is my present stance on the issue of children and harmful actions against them. I do believe that negative situations can be avoided to a large degree by guarding our thoughts. I know that the formula for creation is nonjudgmental and is fueled by emotion. I know that fear and violence are powerful emotions that can create lasting visions in the subconscious.

For this reason you must be careful as you begin to use the creative powers, and guard your thoughts of the negative aspects of life. As your power of creativity grows, your power to attract to you what visions lie in your subconscious does too. Be careful: don't dwell on negativity or tragic events for your own good and the good of people around you. Replace those negative thoughts with positive thoughts as soon as you become aware that you are thinking them. When I have a negative thought that lingers, I project it on the screen of the mind and then I grab the image as if it were a photograph and ball it up. Then I throw it as far away from me as I can.

Karma and Fatalism: Another aspect of negative creation comes up in the misconception of the term karma and the concept of fatalism. "Karma" is a term that is fundamental to the Hindu religion and refers to the basic substance (peanut butter) that creates the fabric of existence over which humans have the power to influence with their mind. "Fatalism" describes the concept that the major events and general course of our lives are predetermined and cannot be changed. European, Christian missionaries misinterpreted karma to mean the receiving of actions in the present life that were a result of actions in a previous life. Thus, karma has been mistakenly equated to fatalism.

The harm in fatalism rises from maintaining the idea that you may experience events in this lifetime, presumably negative, that you did not cause by the thoughts you hold in this lifetime. If this were so, the laws of the universe would be in conflict with karma and fatalism because actions could arise in this lifetime that were out of your direct control as they were not the result of thoughts held in your present consciousness.

Fortunately, Hindu religious leaders view the general idea of karma as generally equivalent to the concept of conscious creativity expressed in this book. The significant difference is that the idea of creative consciousness is not contained within a religious context, while the term karma is fundamental to Hinduism. Both creative consciousness and karma are expressions of the universal laws. Both concepts agree that unresolved issues begun in this lifetime will continue to create and manifest in this life. They also agree that if you accept responsibility for your life, deal with the negative elements of your life and change the thoughts in your subconscious, your life at the objective level will change as well.

When you begin to take an active role in creating the events of your life, the negative events and situations you unknowingly created in the past will begin to lessen and fade away. To avoid future negative events, you must consult with your assistants before beginning each project, and learn to clearly visualize the images you want in your life. Your assistants will offer you invaluable guidance to manage conflicts or negativity in relationships at work or within your family or friends.

Solving problems and setting goals is the reason that you created your workshop and assistants. It is a place for you to find out what you want to create as well as whether or not what you want to create is actually "good" for you. The screen of the mind is the part of your workshop that you created to project your images. Your assistants are your way of accessing the two balancing aspects of your subconscious mind to find out how you personally feel about the projects that you objectively think that you want. They will tell you what it is you really want; be sure to listen to them.

CHAPTER TWENTY-FOUR

Emotion and Goal Setting

Your mind is not strong enough nor is there enough time in a day for you to create everything you can imagine. You should pick a long-term project and a short-term project, accomplish those and move on to other projects. One of the most important aspects of choosing which projects to create is emotion. Emotion should be thought of as energy in motion and is the powerful fuel needed to drive the creative force.

Ideas and images originate in the subjective mind due to our ability to create visions in our mind. We commonly refer to this process as using our imagination. Ideas are free-floating images of possible situations that can be positive or negative, beneficial or harmful, wholesome or macabre. Ideas can come from anywhere and they can be about anything. They can fly through your mind in an instant, they can stay for a moment, form an image and then disappear, or they can form an image that is so compelling that you feel you must have it in your life.

The measure of your desire for an image is measured by the emotion you attach to it. The stronger the desire, the more emotion or creative energy you provide. If you have a clear vision of what you want and strong emotional attachment to the image, it will manifest in your life.

But remember, the process of creative manifestation requires that you take action. As any truly creative person will tell you, being creative is 10 percent inspiration and 90 percent perspiration. So the question is not what you should imagine but what you should do. What appropriate action should you take after you have decided what image you want to create and what goal you want to achieve?

Your assistants will always answer the question of the next appropriate step for you to take. If you follow the directions of your assistants, they will lead you unerringly to your goal. If you accomplish one set of directions from your assistants, go back into your levels and ask what is next, they will give you further directions. Be advised that when you use the formula for creation in your workshop and apply personal action to your vision, you absolutely will go through the experience you imagine. The formula does not know good from bad, nor can it distinguish beneficial desires from harmful desires. As my teacher once said, once you put the formula for creation into action, you will go, kicking and screaming, through the experience. So when creating something in your life, be sure to check with your assistants. They know what you really want and whether or not what you want is in your best interests.

Remember you will not be able to create material things instantly. Some things may take months or years of hard, mental and physical work to accomplish. The truly great works of humankind took many years to conceive and plan and often decades to finish. That is why the strong emotion of desire is essential; it will sustain you as the creative process does its work.

CHAPTER TWENTY-FIVE

Making Your Goals Come to Life

*N*ow that you have all the information needed for the creation of your life, let's go through the process of creation in its entirety and see how it works. I cannot tell you what to create. However, I do know that you will become better at it as you gain experience and confidence in the process.

I recommend that your first conscious creative attempt not be something of a global nature like world peace or the end of poverty. You are, after all, only one person who must mix your consciousness with more than six billion others. Find something that you want to have happen to you personally, or something that you need to locate that seems hard to find, or a favorable reaction from someone with whom you have not yet connected. Keep it simple, keep it personal and do not involve a lot of other people. Do not try something like trying to get everyone in your math class an A. Find something simple, something personal and make sure that it has an emotional value for you. If you have a hard time coming up with something, ask your assistants.

To begin, find a quiet place, close your eyes, relax and review your colors. If you note strong reactions to any colors, be sure to review them with your assistants and correct the imbalances that you feel before beginning your creation. If there are several major imbalances, use this trip to your workshop as a chance to create personal harmony. Do not try to create your life while you are in a state of inner turmoil.

Assuming there is nothing major going on within you at the moment, continue to your relaxing scene and pause there long enough to know that you are relaxed and your breathing is slow and effortless. Continue into your subconscious to your workshop. Enter, greet your assistants and sit in your executive chair. Talk to your assistants and let them know what it is that you want. Ask them if they think this is a good first project. If they agree, sit in your chair, and project a vision of what you want to create on the screen of the mind. Be sure you are personally represented in the vision in such a way that there is no doubt that what you want to create is associated with you. It is possible to create things into your life that are not yours; like wanting money and then being offered a job in a bank. Take time to create a vision that will be effective in achieving the goal you want.

The Perfect End Result. When creating your life, take time to think through project you want to achieve with the help of your assistants. Often a person will strive for a goal and then concentrate on a vision that will not necessarily lead them to where they want to go. The vision of the goal you generate must represent the perfect end of your goal and not some intermediate point.

For example: when I was unmarried, I tried to be witty, charming and make a lot of money because I thought that was what women wanted. I thought that if I had those qualities I would meet a beautiful woman who would be my wife and love me forever.

I tried and tried to be witty, charming and make a lot of money but never seemed to succeed to the level I thought would make me meet the girl of my dreams. My assistants tried to get me to relax and realize that I had not yet developed the qualities necessary for being a good husband. They emphatically pointed out this was what marriage-minded women really wanted.

After much trial and error, I finally envisioned myself walking arm in arm with a beautiful woman in that special way that people in love do. The vision resulted with me being introduced to my future wife on a blind date within six months. She was, and is, beautiful.

We fell in love on the first date and were married seven months later. The only reason we waited so long was because her friends were worried about the type of person I was. I could understand their concern. I had no money, no great job, and could manage to be witty and charming only part of the time. Yet, we love each other and have been as happy as two people can be for the past 20 years. This experience taught me to hold the vision of the perfect end result of what I wanted and let the power of creation work out the details.

If your creative vision involves someone else that you already know, it is always best to call him or her to your workshop for a meeting before making a final decision on what you will do. To get the other person into your workshop, all you have to do is go into your workshop and ask them to appear inside your elevator. Wait a second or two, and when you feel their presence inside the elevator, lower the door and invite them in.

Talk with them just as you normally would. Their communication most likely will be verbal, but also notice their actions, expressions, and body language. Once you find out how they feel about your intentions, you will know whether to continue your project with them, modify it or abandon it. **Never, tell a person at the objective level that you spoke with them in your subconscious.** If you must make reference to your subjective conversations at the objective level, say something like, "I've been thinking about you" or "You've been on my mind."

Subjective "conversations" held in the workshop are more valuable than objective level face-to-face conversations for finding out how a person feels about you or a situation. This is because you and the other person are communicating directly from subjective mind to subjective mind with no social issues in the way. It can be a bit disheartening to experience how some people truly feel about you. The participants do not feel the need to pretend kindness or soften the ideas presented in order not to offend. But there will be others of which you were unaware who offer the gift of true friendship to you and that should be compensation enough. In either case, operating from a basis of truth is best in the long run.

Despite their value, your conclusions reached in your workshop are very hard to justify at the objective level. Rely on the information you receive, but don't openly discuss the information you gather in workshop "conversations" with other people. Just use the things you learn as a guide for your future actions.

Visit your workshop at least once a day to replay your vision. Take time to bring the vision sharply into focus. Be sure to see yourself in the picture in the way you want to be and visualize the outcome you want. Don't worry about the details since they will fall into place as the creative process does its work.

When visualizing a goal, if the vision doesn't appear easily or is not distinctly clear in your mind, stop the creative effort and consult with your assistants. Unclear visions can be the result of many things: lack of desire, personal barriers that exist within your subconscious that need to be removed or lack of a clear understanding of what it is you really want. Whatever the cause, your assistants will know what to do. When you create your vision be sure to get physically active. As you sit in your chair meditating, use your hands, get involved and make the subjective experience as real as you can.

Before leaving your levels, ask your assistants if there are any other actions you should take. If not, say good-bye to your assistants, and leave through the door you entered. Pause a moment under the white light outside the door and feel the energy of the white light entering your body. Ascend out of your deep subconscious level to your relaxing scene in nature, and pause there only briefly as you will already be relaxed from meditative state. Find your pathway to the objective level. Climb up the 12 rungs of the stairs or ladder or up 12 floors in an elevator, and arrive at the level of your colors. See the colors in reverse order: violet, purple, blue, green, yellow, orange and red. When seeing the color red, open your eyes and feel refreshed and confident that what you are creating is on its way.

CHAPTER TWENTY-SIX

Receiving Answers

When you use your workshop and assistants to create your life, you may not only want to create objects. You may have questions or problems you want your assistants to resolve for you. They will certainly be able to help you because they have direct access to the universal mind. However, finding the answer may take time because the universe does not always feel the need to act or deliver your creations in the time or fashion that you expect.

The time required before the answer comes depends upon you and the question. Many times your assistants will have the answer for you immediately. Other times they will let you know that the answer will take some time. Your concept of time may be different than the concept of time for your assistants so be patient. I generally receive answers within three days, but you may have a different experience.

How you receive the answer may take many forms. You may be talking to someone unrelated to the problem, see a billboard, look at a cloud or stare off into space, and an answer will suddenly pop into your conscious mind. During the discussion of awareness in Chapter Twelve, I mentioned the idea of you expanding your awareness of the events at the objective level. I did this because oftentimes the answers you seek are keyed into your objective consciousness by something you become aware of. Looking at a stoplight, for example, and realizing that you need to pay the electricity bill, or looking at the network of branches on a leafless tree and having the solution to a networking problem you are having at work suddenly pop into your mind. The point is to be aware of your need to look into your immediate environment as well as your subconscious for the answers to the problems you face. The environment, per se, may not have the answer, but the environment may make the connection with the answer to your problem that is trying to reach you from your subjective mind.

One of the best keys to creativity and goal achievement is to listen to your assistants guiding you from within. Listening to your assistants is easy; the hard part is finding a time to do it. As you recall from the discussions of the mind in Chapter Eleven, your brain operates like a computer. Computers can do only one task at a time. They may appear to perform more than one task at a time but actually they duplex; that is, they switch from one task to another rapidly so the two events get blurred together. But in the final analysis computers and your brain, can process only one instruction at a time. This relates directly to receiving answers from your assistants in a surprising way.

Your assistants work at the subjective level to find answers and can give the answers to you either in your workshop or at the objective level as you go about your day. The trouble is that the conscious mind cannot always receive the answers your assistants find because your brain is already busy doing other tasks. As long as you require your brain to perform tasks that require instructions to flow **into** your brain (work, music, television, or chitchat with your friends), your assistants cannot push the answers you asked for **out of** your subconscious mind into your objective level of mind. In order to listen to the subjective part of your mind, your objective mind must be somewhat inactive. Simply put, you need to *learn to be still* and listen to yourself. If you want to receive the solutions to the problems you asked your assistants to solve you've got to make time to receive them.

All humankind, the great and the ordinary, have received flashes of insight, epiphanies, flashes of genius, creative visions or whatever you want to call them, to solve problems on which they were working. Albert Einstein struggled with the problems of the relationship of the speed of light and time - Special Relativity, as he called it - for years before the final answer came to him. After years of walking and talking about the problem with his friends in the city parks in Berne, Switzerland, the solution Einstein sought for so long came to him in a flash of understanding from within.

One day, as he and one of his friends, Michele Besso, were walking in a park, the logic of the relativity of time flashed like a lightning bolt into his mind. Einstein, fearful of losing the solution, abruptly ran back to his apartment rather than discuss it with his friend. Far into the night he wrote down his revelations while they were fresh in his mind. The next day he reported to his friend that he had finally solved the entire problem. Besso, Einstein's unassuming sounding board, was delighted that his friend Albert had finally found the solution they had sought for so long. So if you want to be a genius, you must start acting like one and create time for the answers you seek to come into your mind. Keeping a notepad and a pencil handy to record the information is a good idea too.

To use your subjective level of mind and your assistants to solve problems, you must find a time of day, or several times of day, when they can report to you. Personally, I find that if I turn off the radio as I drive, the solitude of the car is enough to allow my assistants to reach me. Make no mistake, I love popular music, but there are things that are more important. Walking is good too. Many a good argument has gone on in my head as I walked. I seem to be functioning in the here and now as I walk, but actually my body is on autopilot and my assistants and I are a million miles away working hard on some issue. I guess it looks strange to other people to see a grown man walking along, gesturing and mumbling under his breath, but it works. I see other people doing the same thing; I never laugh because I respect the value of their inner dialogue.

Before we end our discussion on creation, I should pass along an important point. Never limit your power creativity. If you have something that you feel strongly about, something that comes with strong emotion, go for it. **Do not stop and try to "figure out" with your objective brain what your subjective mind is capable of.** Allowing your objective mind to determine your creative limits is like allowing a six-year-old child to tell you how to drive. If you do fall into this trap, you will be governed by your fears and doubts rather than your true creative abilities.

CHAPTER TWENTY-SEVEN

Dream Killers

*A*s all of us know, fear and doubt are emotions that are just as real as courage and knowledge. But instead of taking us upward fear and doubt hold us back. I can assure you from hard experience that whenever you start to create and achieve something that you feel is important, other people who do not share your vision, emotion or perspective will downplay or openly ridicule your idea.

This tendency for humans to ridicule what they don't understand is a human trait that usually surrounds people who are unaware of the creative process. It is hard to recall an inventor, humanitarian, or innovator, who hasn't suffered the negative thoughts of small-minded people. Some of your "friends" will tell you they are only trying to look out for your best interests, but usually it is a control mechanism designed, knowingly or unknowingly, to get you to do only what they think is possible.

Whatever their motive, you must learn to press on, without their approval, with what you believe to be worthwhile. Remember there will **always** be people who feel the need to put out the emotional fire of your projects. By the way, you should be aware that when you start to work on an exciting project, you too will personally create an opportunity to quit. It seems that the best projects take a major re-tasking of your subjective creativity effort. Before your subjective mind takes the new project seriously, it will create an opportunity for you to back out. Think of it as an internal sincerity check. You will always be offered a piece of your favorite pie, with ice cream, the very day you decide to go on a diet.

CHAPTER TWENTY-EIGHT

Resolve and Courage

*T*here are two qualities you must develop when taking creative control of your life. These qualities are resolve and courage. You must be strong in your resolve when you start a new project in order to achieve your goal. Once the new project is underway and you see it beginning to manifest, the project will gather energy of its own, especially if like-minded people share the vision of your project. But until that happens, when the project is new and still in a developing state, a strong sense of resolve is required to get and keep the ball rolling.

The world is full of people with good ideas who lack the grit and determination to see a project through to its end. This is especially true if the project requires internal changes and several years to accomplish. Don't go after a goal that does not carry a strong charge of emotion because it is the emotion that creates the resolve. And resolve is essential to see the project through and achieve your goal.

Courage is the other essential quality. Courage is the ability to face your fears. Courage is required when you first start a project because you are not certain that your project will actually manifest. Fear of failure, fear of ridicule, fear of financial loss, and uncertainty as to the validity of the creative process will all be present to sap your emotional energy. If you are to be successful in achieving your

ou must be able to put your fears aside and press
l. Courage in creating your life is essential because many of our meaningful accomplishments take us into the realm of the unknown where we are unsure of the outcome.

Fear is nothing more than the measure of our ignorance. Yet this is no light matter because in the realm of the unknown, fear not courage is the dominant human response. I can remember as if it were yesterday when I was an instructor pilot for the US Navy. We flew the T-28, a single engine, WWII era, propeller driven aircraft. The T-28 was renowned for its spin characteristics because it was so unpredictable. No matter how well trained or courageous the student pilot was, the first flight that required spin recovery in the T-28 was traumatic. Even the good students who normally went through the routine part of the flight with ease were shaky.

As we climbed up to our spin entry altitude, I would review the entry and recovery procedures with them. When we reached the proper altitude, the pilot would report the checklist of spin procedures to me over the intercom. There was no levity or confidence in the student's voice, only the measured monotone of a person who is afraid and about to deal with it. The student would close the throttle; slow the plane to stall speed, nose held high. As the stall speed approached, with wings held level, a rudder pedal was kicked hard over. Then all hell would break loose. The aircraft would shudder, shake and groan as the final elements of lift were shaken from the wings, and then fall in a spin towards the ground like a brick.

All planes of this type spun differently. Some slipped gently off on a wing as the nose fell through into the ever-tightening spin. Others resisted the spin for a second and then bucked almost over on their back as the spin developed. It was a wild ride for sure as the plane bounced and shook, and we were tossed against our seat harness. Sometimes the canopy rattled open an inch or so, and the ground spun in front of us like a map twirling in a whirlwind. The spin became tighter and steeper and the plane buffeted as the wide-eyed student and me in the back seat fell to earth.

The student held the plane into the spin with full rudder and full back stick. When the time came to recover, the student had to do what all his instincts told him not to do. He had to push the stick forward and kick in opposite rudder. This was counterintuitive because the plane was already steeply nose down, the ground below was all we could see, and pushing the stick forward seemed like the last thing to do.

But illogical as it seemed, that was the only way to recover from the spin. The wing was stalled, and we had to get air flowing back over the wings so that we could fly again. Pushing the nose into the relative wind was the only way to end the stall; opposite rudder stopped the rotation. The problem was that the plane did not instantly respond when the spin correction was applied; in fact for about another full turn the spin got more violent. The students would put in the right correction but it wouldn't work immediately.

The students had two choices at this point. They could react to their fear-driven survival instincts and pull the stick back in a vain attempt to raise the nose, which would only make the aircraft continue to stall and spin, or they could trust the spin recovery procedures, keep the nose down and opposite rudder in until the rotation stopped. Once the rotation stopped, the student neutralized the controls, raised the nose back to the horizon, added power and flew away none the worse for the experience.

The procedures always worked, and reverting to fear-driven instincts never did. Courage was summoned, fears overcome, a lesson was learned, and experience gained, all in less than a minute. After their first spin recovery flight, the students walked a little easier, relaxed a little more. There was still much more training to do, but because they had overcome their fear of the spin and gained confidence, the path to earning their wings was a little easier.

So, you too must learn to trust the process of creation and believe in the formula. As you grow more experienced with the process, you will gain the confidence you need to start new projects without the burden of fear. However, you will never gain confidence without positive experience. My teacher once told me that expecting confidence without having experience is like telling a fireplace, "If you keep me warm, I'll put wood in you." The process doesn't work that way.

Remember, courage is the ability to face your fears, and fear is the measure of your ignorance. In order to overcome ignorance you must act with courage and face your fear. Even at my age I continue to test my courage and try something that scares the pants off of me. The result for me is a renewed sense of confidence and a heighten appreciation of life.

Another note of caution, do not use the formula for creation as a crutch to avoid doing the work of creation. If you have a big history exam tomorrow or a presentation at work, never delude yourself by trusting your assistants to dig up the answers for you out of the universal mind without preparation. The answers are there but it may take awhile for your assistants to get them. Meanwhile your window of performance has come and gone. It is far better to prepare objectively for the "tests" in your life and then relax knowing that you have put the information you need in your short-term memory where your assistants can easily find it during the exam. If, at the outset, you begin using the formula as an adolescent trick to avoid your responsibilities, you will find that Law II will most certainly apply and the people in your life will begin to avoid their responsibilities to you.

Therefore, use your workshop and the formula for creation wisely. Remember, most desires, (not all), take some amount of time before they manifest. Don't forget that your workshop can be used for many things other than the creation of objects such as problem solving, heart-to-heart conversations, relationships, healing and confidence building.

CHAPTER TWENTY-NINE

Doing a Case

*I*n your workshop, with the help of your assistants, you can interview people, develop a feeling for the impact of your present actions on the future, resolve personal conflicts and aid in healing people. Healing people is what I call "doing a case." You don't have to be a doctor or act like a doctor to do a case. All you have to do is call the person who needs a case done into your workshop and do whatever your assistants tell you to do in order to aid in the healing process.

There's a special place in the workshop for healing. When doing a case it is not necessary to know the medical definition of the person's condition. I believe that knowing the medical term for an "illness" may be a hindrance because it predisposes me to think of the situation in only one way.

For example, you may hear that a person has cancer and call them to your workshop to treat their cancer. This, unfortunately, may not be the best course of action. In fact, it may not be what they really need to make them well. Medical miracles abound; there are volumes of research published to support the idea that humans are capable of healing themselves. What they need to accomplish the healing is the power to believe it. The case you do can help provide them the extra energy they need to take care of their own health by attacking the root cause of the illness and not the specific illness itself.

The following case is a hypothetical example of what you might do in your workshop to facilitate healing. Your experience may be different from my example in many ways; certainly no two cases are alike. But what ever you do in the spirit of service will be beneficial.

First invite the person into your workshop via the elevator. Ask them to stand in the medical assistance area of your workshop and make an their own assessment of the cause of their condition. Remain nonjudgmental during their "diagnosis." Do not resist their assessment of their condition in any way. Once you have heard how they feel, ask them if there is a service you can provide or any assistance they need from you. If they have a request, give them what they ask for. If they want to be hugged, hug them. If they want a relaxing day at the beach, create a car or airplane from your tools, visualize a beach scene, get in and take a trip to the beach.

Second, act on your subjective understanding of their condition by doing whatever you feel compelled to do to help them. Give them a green tee shirt to wear under their clothes to give them achieve a sense of peace. Or paint their hair with blue paint, (there will be a can of it in just the right color in the materials area of your workshop) to let them know love surrounds them. This may seem silly but it works if YOU believe it will. The colors represent energy forms and an increase of energy for them in the universal mind will release their own healing energy so they can cure themselves.

Every case I have done would seem ridiculous at the objective level. But I do cases anyway, silly seeming or not, because I know they work. I have dedicated my life to being of service to my fellow human beings in the best way I know how. To that end, I sincerely want to aid any person who needs assistance. And, as silly seeming as a case is, I know they work and it's all I know how to do to be of service.

The important thing to remember is that a medical diagnosis is not necessary to do a case. What is necessary is to give the person needing assistance what they tell you they need and what you subjectively feel they need. When doing a case always project an image of their complete recovery on the screen of the mind for you both to see while you have them in your workshop. They should depart through the elevator when they are ready to leave.

Doing a case is another instance where use of the creative process is best kept secret. I never discuss the cases I do with anyone, especially the person on which I do a case. I do what I can and know with absolute certainty that my efforts will help them achieve the perfect end result for them. I never forget that helping to heal another person is not something I feel personally capable of doing. The power to heal is contained in the power of Law I. When I do a case, I am only adding my healing consciousness to the universal mind where the person who needs positive energy can make use of it. This does not seem like much but the results can be dramatic, even "miraculous."

Do not allow doing a case to be a substitute for seeking medical assistance, taking prescribed medications or following the advice of those in the healing professions. View a case as one more weapon in the battle of restoring a person's good health. Doing a case is a way to be of true service to humanity, and you should not hesitate to do one if the need arises.

The creation of situations, material objects or healing, sets a series of events in motion that benefit not only you but also the world as a whole. As you will learn in the next chapter, the benefits to humankind from the creative acts of individuals are far-reaching and essential to our continued survival as a species.

CHAPTER THIRTY

The Ultimate Benefit

side from creating a successful life, just the way you want it, there are unexpected benefits to be had from engaging in the process of creation. These benefits are a true serendipity not only to you but also to all humankind. The most important benefit has far reaching implications for the future of humanity on earth. Most people don't think that long-term. But as every science teacher knows, we must look far ahead sometimes because time is running out for us humans here on earth and we need to begin to act now.

Change is the constant force that reshapes the universe. Life on Earth is the result of a series of unimaginably complex conditions that undergo constant change as our solar system changes. The key to our survival is water in the liquid phase. Inevitable changes in the composition of the sun will eventually create the conditions here on Earth that will cause water, the source of life, to slowly evaporate.

The Sun emits light throughout the solar system as the result of the fission/fusion reaction of energized hydrogen, the Sun's primary element. The explosion that takes place during this fission/fusion reaction is what causes the Sun to shine. In the distant future, approximately four billion years from now the result of the fusion of hydrogen into helium and helium into other heavier elements will cause the Sun to expand. This will happen because the increase in dense matter in the core of the Sun will cause it to retain more of its energy. As the Sun becomes denser, it will become hotter and expand. It will expand slowly but inevitably to such an extent that, in time, it will engulf Mercury, Venus and Earth, the three planets closest to it. But long before that, who can say exactly when, the Sun will expand and grow so hot that the Earth will be unable to sustain liquid water. When that happens, all the creatures on Earth must perish, including humans

We are in a unique position to save ourselves because in the time before the conditions that sustain life on Earth disappear, we can use our powers of creativity and find a way to move to another home in a different part of the universe. I know this sounds a little sci-fi and far out, but it is true. We can't stay on Earth forever so we must find a place to go and way to leave. We must leave Earth and a find a new planet to call home if we want to survive. The question is, can we do it?

The answer lies in our ability to increase our creative, problem- solving ability. Like it or not, believe it or not, the future of all humanity depends upon our ability to increase our creative powers and pass them along to those who come after us. We must do this so that humankind can survive in the future.

In order for humankind to exist in the future, we must develop our creative powers here and now. If we do this, those who follow us can build on what we have learned. It is important, therefore, that we learn to tap into our creative ability, use the universal mind and benefit the future by living more creatively in the present. Only by developing our creative powers can we demonstrate our full potential as human beings to our children and, thereby, transfer it to the future. Then the power of creativity, increased as it is passed along through generation after generation, will allow humankind to receive the ultimate benefit of survival and find a new place to live and perpetuate itself.

I don't know why we have been given the power to save ourselves and not perish along with the rest of the creatures on earth. I only know that we have the power to do it if we choose to use it. In the final analysis, we have no choice. It is either become more creative and pass it along to our children, or perish.

In the everyday world of today, the benefits of using our creative powers are much easier to understand. They will be evident all around us as we begin to use the process and create our life. Benefits will come to you even as the process of creation is in progress. They can be enjoyed before the object of your creation is manifest.

CHAPTER THIRTY-ONE

Fear-Based Creations

A s with any other human activity: learning to drive or fly, there are negative situations that come up as you begin a new venture. They are nothing terrible but need to be explained beforehand so you will have an idea of what to expect during some aspects of the early stages of your creative efforts.

One temporary problem that arises is that creations from your past visions and fears, rather than from your new set of visions, will continue to create situations in your life. They will run their course and eventually stop all together as the new, conscious, process takes hold. How long that takes depends upon each individual. The creations stemming from your past fears and negativity, sickness, theft, accidents, unsatisfying relationships, etc, will continue as your subconscious clears out the fear-based creations that were in the works before you began to take control of the process.

Remember the story of the student pilot and the spin recovery process in a previous chapter? It will be the same for you. You must learn the process, apply the process and then have the courage to wait for the process to take full control. "Negative" or "bad" things may still occur in your life, but they will occur less and less frequently as time goes by and the process takes hold. Consciousness cleansing does not mean that your new goals won't manifest too. It's just that the fear-based creations, for a time, will manifest as well.

As surprising as it may seem, there is a part of your mind that does not want you to change to a positively oriented, consciousness-controlled way of life. This is so because the subconscious mind has so much invested in the operation of the old, objective reality-based way of life that it doesn't want to change its way of operating to the reality of the subconscious-based way of life unless it is sure that the changes it must go through to make the adjustment will be permanent. To overcome this inner resistance, you must re-task your mind through repeated application of the creative process in your levels. You must show it that you mean business and never intend to revert to the objective-level action/reaction way of life.

I have practiced the subconscious based way of living my life for over 25 years and I have experienced many wonderful and exciting things. But every now and then I still occasionally experience what I call fear-based manifestations. These are unpleasant aggressive thoughts from others to me or from me to others or actions such as accidents, personal confrontations, near misses in traffic, health problems or anything else that makes me feel anxious, afraid or out of tune with my life. I am disturbed by these events because I know that they are not accidents. They happened because of thoughts or fears I have in my subconscious. I know that unless I deal with the problem at the subjective level it will continue to manifest in my life.

When negative, fear-based events occur, I go to my levels, consult with my assistants and determine the basis for the fear that caused the manifestation. Then I do my best to deal with the fear that caused the manifestation. I take time to learn what it is I'm afraid of and experience the fear if I feel the need. I overcome, as well as I can, the ignorance that caused the fear. I have realized I cannot deal with fear by ignoring it or telling myself that the fear will go away by itself. I know it won't. In order for you to conquer your fears you must have the honesty to accept the fears you feel and the courage to face them head on. You must remember that fear is the result of ignorance, not knowing something. You must generate the strength and courage to overcome the ignorance that causes fear with knowledge.

Intellectualizing: The quickest and surest way to gain the knowledge to overcome fear is by experience. A person who is afraid cannot overcome their fears by talking about them. Talking about something rather than doing something is called intellectualizing. Intellectualizing is mental activity that takes the place of acquiring real life experience.

People who intellectualize their problems don't actually do anything to end them; they just talk about them. Intellectualizing is what people do until they can gather the courage to experience what it is they are afraid of. For example, in order to overcome a fear of snakes, someone must find a person who owns a snake and make a visit to find out what snakes are really like. To truly overcome the fear of snakes you will have to hold a snake or pet one and talk with the owner of the snake to find out what snakes do and how they live.

When dealing with fear, actions speak louder than words. Only when you have a real experience with what you fear can you gain the knowledge you need to overcome the fear. Intellectualizing, that is talking about your fear, or thinking about overcoming fear will never work because these activities do not supply the deeply felt understanding that is required to overcome fear; only real life experience can do that for sure. If you fail to address your fears and overcome them they will haunt you until you do.

CHAPTER THIRTY-TWO

Being in the Process

*A*s you begin to apply the goal achievement process to your life, you will begin to experience several improvements almost immediately. Once you have achieved a goal or had a positive experience that you are certain you created you begin to change from inside. The changes are an inevitable benefit to using the creative process.

Stress Reduction: The first thing you will notice is that your stress level will drop. For the first time in your life you will be able to relax and stop trying so hard. As time passes and you continue to practice the goal achievement process, your physical health will improve, you will meet new friends, destructive relationships will pass, fears will lessen, and you will emerge as a happier, more self-confident person. Application of the creative process is always satisfying and more pleasurable than just drifting along. It is a wonderful feeling to know that you, and only you, are in control of your life.

Another important benefit of conscious creation is that when you begin a project you know you will complete, you begin to acquire the same feelings of confidence, satisfaction and inner peace you would have if you had already completed the project. In other words, the pay-off for personal creation is that you begin to feel the peace and confidence of the goal you will accomplish while you are in the process of its creation and do not have to wait until the project is complete.

Many successful people I have known have told me that the best part of their projects was how they felt in the development stages and not how they felt when the project was complete. Many expressed feeling a sort of emptiness on the day their goals were reached. I know I felt that way when I graduated from college and when I got my Navy flight wings. It seems that being "in the process," no matter how difficult it becomes, provides a sense of purpose and wellbeing that ends when the project is complete. To get the feeling again, you have to begin to create something new. The feeling of being "in the process" is enough motivation for even the most successful people to keep on being creative and moving ahead with their lives.

Character Development: The most significant benefit from use of the creative process is the development of personal character. Developing character means developing inner qualities such as honesty, humility, forth rightfulness, respect, integrity and courtesy. My personal definition of character is encompassed by what I call the three Rs.

As a middle school teacher, I was puzzled by the traditional use of the 3-Rs to describe the goals of education. First, the 3-Rs referred to reading, writing and arithmetic. I could not see how educated people could come up with the 3-Rs from an R, a W and an A. Surely, I thought, the educated people of America could come up with a more profound statement to encompass their educational philosophy than something based upon the backwoods pronunciations of "readin, 'ritin, and 'rithmetic." I did not think that this folksy summation of the goals of education reflected my own goals for my students, so I decided to create my own.

After about five minutes of reflection I came up with my own 3-Rs. My 3-Rs were based upon my feelings that the goal of education should be character development and not solely the acquisition of academic skill sets. Respect, Responsibility and Results were the 3-Rs I came up with. I cut these three words out of construction paper and hung them over the marker board at the head of my class.

In my opinion, educated people should develop the character to respect one another above all else. Educated people should develop sufficient character to take personal responsibility for their conduct and performance. Educated people, as the result of their education, should develop the character to expect to accomplish a goal that is of benefit to society. The acquisition of knowledge is supposed to create the vision of a worthy goal in their minds that they were expected to achieve.

The self-education you are about to undergo will require the same goals from you. If you decide to apply the process of creation to your life and reap the benefits, you will be required to develop your character and accomplish a worthy goal. Character development, by the way, is not optional; as it is a byproduct of the creative process.

Law I causes character development because it requires that you create only those thoughts (visions for yourself) that you already hold in consciousness. What this means is that when you set out to create something, you must already hold in your deep subconscious a vision of what it is you want to possess. Not only must you hold the vision of what you want, but you must believe that you are worthy of attaining your vision. If you visualize something you have not developed the character to have, you must develop that character before you can have it. This means that in order to have something, you must either possess or develop, at the subconscious level, the character that thing or position requires.

Acceptance of Visions: I first encountered the concept of acceptance of visions in the classic book, *Jonathan Livingston Seagull*. The author, Richard Bach, used the allegory of a seagull, Jonathan, who attempts to become an expert, fast-flying seagull, to present the concept of Law I to his readers. Jonathan wants to fly as fast as it is possible for a gull to go. It turns out that Jonathan's efforts to fly as fast as possible are limited by his ideas that fast flight is a function of the physical configuration of his wings and his speed diving technique. His teacher, Chiang the elder gull, tells Jonathan that the trick of traveling at the ultimate speed is being able to travel at the speed of thought. Chiang describes the speed of thought this way: "To fly as fast as thought, to anywhere that is" Chiang said, "You must begin by knowing that you have already arrived." Those 10 words form the basis for all the creative efforts of humankind.

Knowing that you have already arrived means that you have developed a creative vision to the point that you have accepted the vision of your goal as yours. You already know, not merely believe, that what is in your vision will manifest in your life. Law I states clearly that you must hold the vision in consciousness as something you truly know you deserve and not just believe, wish or hope you do. When you wish or hope for something its a clear indication that you don't have it.

Positive Thinking: Wishing and hoping are forms of a widespread method of self-deception called positive thinking. Positive thinking, in the context of this book, does not mean having a bright, happy outlook on life. Positive thinking, in this context, is a false sense of security. It comes from thinking at the objective level that harmful or negative ideas you hold at the subjective level might not actually turn out to be harmful.

Positive thinking is the epitome of immature, wishful thinking. Positive thinking is the opposite of aware thinking. Aware thinking is not thinking everything will be all right no matter what you do. Aware thinking means taking action to do all that you can to ensure that everything will be all right. It means being aware of your physical surroundings and holding an inner vision of what you want to have happen at the objective level.

For an extreme example, assume a person has fallen off a ship in the middle of the ocean. While treading water, a positive thinker would say, "Oh, everything is going to turn out fine. Soon the captain will realize that I have fallen off the ship and will order the ship to turn around and save me." At the subjective level, the person in the water does not really feel that things will turn out fine. Probably he is not sure the captain knows he fell overboard and is terrified, wanting desperately not to die. The positive thinker is afraid to die but he has not made the slightest attempt to deal with his fear.

On the other hand, the aware person who falls overboard probably feels precisely the same as the positive thinker but reacts to the situation differently. While treading water, he goes into his levels and tells his assistants that he is terrified and wants to be saved. The assistants will ask the person to counteract his fear with a clear vision of being safely back on board the boat. The difference is that the aware, creative person knows he is in a desperate situation, admits his fear and takes all possible actions to create a positive conclusion to the situation. The positive thinker suppresses his fear by saying that nothing bad is going to happen and that everything will be all right.

While this example is a bit dramatic, it makes the point that just saying or thinking that bad things won't happen will not prevent them from happening. Your life is not a result of what you think you would like to have happen but rather the result of your deeply held visions for yourself. You must take control and create a positive vision of the desired end result of what you wish to have manifest.

Because goal achievement must include character development, the issues you decide to use to develop your character should always be left to you and your assistants to decide. They know you, your capabilities and what you believe about yourself. They know what you really want and what elements of character you need to develop. Therefore only you should ultimately decide what to do when setting your goals. This is not meant to say that you should not listen to advice from people you love and trust. But in the final analysis you alone need to decide the course of your life, not your friends, family or the latest fad. If you ask other people whether or not you should achieve a goal, they will respond with *their* fears, motivations and character flaws in mind, rather than yours.

For example, let's say your assistants ask you to become a high-wire walker in a circus as part of your character development towards a larger goal. Your friends may be terrified of heights and the idea of becoming a high wire performer is terrifying to them and wasteful of a "perfectly good education." They will, therefore, try to dissuade you from your project because it doesn't fit within their own experiences and comfort level. However, learning to walk the high wire may be just the thing you need do to overcome a lack of courage.

Your assistants know that you have to learn to face your fears. Your assistants will have undoubtedly assessed your character in view of your long-range goal and decided this would be the perfect way to develop the courage you need to reach your goal. Though meaning to be helpful, friends may unknowingly provide information from their limited perspective that will dissuade you from attempting a goal that you could achieve if you worked at it. Listen to your friends, but check the advice you receive from them with your assistants. Your assistants know you better than anybody else; let them guide your way.

I remember a man who followed in his father's footsteps and went to Harvard University, and then on Harvard Medical School to study medicine. He was bright, studied hard and eventually became a doctor. When I met him, he was no longer a doctor. He had given up his profession and was in the process of finding some other occupation. My curiosity overcame me, and I asked him why, after all those years of study and expense, he quit being a doctor. His reply astounded me. He said he found the practice of medicine confining and he did not like to work indoors around sick people. He saw them, for the most part, to be ill-tempered whiners and unpleasant to deal with. If he had known what you know now he could have checked with his assistants before deciding to go to medical school and discovered whether he was truly motivated to be a doctor.

Time Delays: The interval between when we envision something and when it actually manifests in our life is called a time delay. In most cases you will not be able to instantly have what you envision. The delay in time between what you want for yourself and when it gets here will not limit your ability to create but will, in some cases, slow, the process.

Time delays are a way of preventing harm to others and us by visions that are not well thought out. If you think about it, we would get into big trouble if we were able to have every vision or desire manifest immediately, especially if we did not have the wisdom or the experience to foresee the full impact of our thoughts on all those affected by our actions. If we had that perspective we would be God or god-like and we are not gods. Time delays are needed because we mortals lack the infinite perspective of the creator.

For example, the frustration of rush hour traffic sometimes causes me to want to "strangle" the driver ahead of me who is reading the newspaper as he drives in stop-and-go rush hour traffic. I think he should put the paper aside and pay attention to his driving. The driver's sluggish response to the car ahead of him and his lack of concern for the smooth flow of traffic makes me crazy with impatience. Believe me, I do not want to harm a soul on this Earth. But for an instant, my anger and frustration create a violent vision of me wringing the driver's neck. In a less frustrating moment I am aware that the violent, fingers-around-the-neck vision is more destructive to me than to the driver because the violence that I am projecting to him is not the sort of thing I want to see coming back to me. And, according to Law II, it will if I continue to give my vision emotional energy.

It is at this moment that I am grateful for the time delay factor in creative goal achievement. The time delay factor in vision manifestation keeps me from doing harm to others and thereby myself. So, sometimes it's good to have a delay so that you can do your internal check with your assistants and find out the best way to handle the frustration you feel. It is the universe's way of saying, "Are you really sure that you want this for yourself?"

By the way, history has recorded people who had the ability to rapidly create from their visions, so it is not impossible. But, for the vast majority of humanity, the time delay exists and instant creations are out of reach. Thank goodness they are since I truly would not want to hurt anyone even if I could.

CHAPTER THIRTY-THREE

Challenge Yourself

Many of the people I have met who have been successful in their lives have undertaken some challenging task or overcome a difficult barrier early in their life. Overcoming a barrier or meeting a challenge developed their character because they had to use courage to overcome the fear inherent in the challenge. So if you are young and unsure of yourself, or if you are in a rut and life seems flat or unexciting, take on a challenge, do something that you are afraid to do and test your courage. Go sky diving, white water rafting, rock climbing, take up SCUBA diving, learn to fly, enroll in college; test yourself in some way that you feel is a challenge. The courage you need to overcome fear always produces self-confidence. The confidence you develop from overcoming your fears is a significant key to living a successful life.

Barriers: Courage and self-confidence are essential to creating a successful life because they give us the power to confront the barriers that lie between what we are and what we want. The barriers that prevent us from knowing we can achieve our visions are, believe it or not, self-imposed. Barriers are self-imposed because they arise from the fears that we hold in our subconscious and are not permanent in the objective sense. Since barriers arise from fears and fears arise from ignorance, barriers are an excellent method of self-assessment. The power to overcome barriers can be generated in your workshop with your assistants.

Going to your workshop and projecting a vision of the situation that contains the barrier on the screen of the mind is the first step to overcoming a barrier. Do not begin by denying that the barrier exists; that's another example of the destructive power of positive thinking. Also do not begin working to overcome a barrier by telling yourself it is all in your mind and therefore not real. The fact that it is in your mind makes it real.

There is an old saying that goes, "The start to finding a solution to a problem begins by calling it by its right name." If you have a barrier, you must admit to yourself that it exists or you can't overcome it. Create a vision of yourself with the barrier firmly in place. Then once you have the vision connecting you with the barrier and have accepted that this is the way you are, you can change it. Acknowledging and accepting of your barriers prior to changing them is an important point because you can't change what isn't yours.

I once smoked cigarettes. I smoked from the time I was 15 until the time I was about 32. Despite all the information I learned about the health risks and encouragement from my friends, I could not stop smoking. I tried 50 times to stop, and much to my disgust, I would always start up again. Then I went to the "Progressions" class I mentioned in the Introduction and learned about how to overcome barriers.

I went to my levels and told my assistants that I had a barrier to my health that I needed to overcome. I let my subconscious project a true vision of how I really felt about smoking on the screen of the mind and was surprised at what I saw. The vision revealed my true opinion about smoking, which was considerably different than what I thought I felt.

I saw myself using smoking, as bad as it was for me, in many beneficial ways. When I began smoking, I saw it as a way to assert my independence. I saw it as a way to show the world I had become a man and smoked like other men. I saw it as a way to take a break from my present activity. "I need to take a smoke break." I saw it as a way to structure time with other people. "Let's go have a cigarette." I saw it as a way to make contact with other people. "Excuse me, can I bum a match. What brand do you smoke?" I saw it as a way to gather my thoughts and, most importantly, I saw it as a way to reduce stress. What I learned was that, despite the fact that it was physically harmful to me, I enjoyed smoking and did it for a lot of very good reasons.

However, I had made up my mind to quit smoking, and I did. It was much easier than I thought and contained none of the frustrations of the past attempts. All I did was tell my assistants I was aware of the pros and cons of smoking and, all things considered, I had decided to quit. My assistants asked me to choose a date about six months in the future that would be a target date for quitting. The day had to be personally significant to me, so I chose my birthday. Then my assistants told me not to resist the fact that I was a smoker and to rely on what they were going to do to cause the change. They insisted that I was to smoke every time I wanted to and not to objectively "try" to quit. Then they did a case on me. They worked on my brain. I watched in my levels as they "pulled out" the circuit boards that contained the "beneficial" programs regarding smoking and created a vision of me experiencing my life with all the benefits of smoking attained in ways other than by smoking.

I followed their advice and went on enjoying smoking, but was sure to project the new vision of my life without smoking whenever I visited my levels. Several days before my birthday I noticed that the desire to have a cigarette had completely left me. I thought back and realized I had not smoked for three or four days prior to that. When I made the realization that I had stopped, I remember saying "I have three more days until the quit date, so why not light up?" This was the internal sincerity check. I said "no thanks" to the thought of continuing smoking and was done with it. The smoking habit had completely left me; it was as though I had never smoked and is was something I would never consider again. The barrier to my health had vanished. The whole idea that I had ever smoked or would ever smoke left me entirely never to return. I haven't had a cigarette since that day.

Whether you want to quit smoking, end addictions, lose weight or stand up to your overbearing boss is up to you. What is important to make clear is that **all** barriers to achievement, no matter how firmly entrenched they may seem, are self-imposed and can be overcome with acceptance of the old and new visions of your life. You are a person with great powers; you can do anything you decide to do but you'll never know it unless you try. Don't forget, whenever you overcome barriers and face your fears, you improve your character and become a better person.

If you use the creative process you will certainly have to give up some things: You will have to give up poverty, ill health, dead end jobs, boredom, bad relationships, addictions, ignorance, fear and low self esteem. Personally, I can't think of a better way to spend my life than improving myself and making myself a better person.

By becoming better, I do not mean perfect. I have been honestly working at this process for many years, and my family and co-workers can attest that I am far from perfect. But perfection is not the goal. Self-improvement is the goal.

If I were asked to state the purpose of life, I would say without hesitation that it is self-improvement. What is self-improvement? It is the honest attempt to be a better person when I leave this world than when I arrived.

CHAPTER THIRTY-FOUR

The Trap of Materialism

*A*s you begin to use the formula for creation, you will naturally begin to create space for more material things. Working for "stuff" is part of the game of life, especially in the technologically advanced societies of the west. Moderation or temperateness is not a requirement of the use of your creative powers. But material possessions need to be put into perspective.

In our western culture, many of us place an inappropriate value on objects. Society as a whole tends to judge people who have imported cars, big houses and fashionable clothes to be better people than those who have less. No doubt, fine homes, cars, clothes, and accessories are comforting to possess, but they are only a partial measure of the person who possesses them. We tend to overlook, because it is harder to see, that the true value of a human being is not what they have but what they are.

Also be aware that even though material goods are nice to own they come at a price. The material objects you own also own you. Cars require maintenance, insurance, tires and gas; houses are even more difficult and time consuming to maintain. You can acquire all the material objects you can afford but the cost of having them is usually far greater than the initial price tag.

If you are not ready or able to devote your mental and physical resources to maintain the things you own, chaos will set in and they will begin to fall to disrepair. Anything you have created will require a sincere effort on your part to maintain. The effort required to maintain the material objects will put a drain on your time and energy. The time and energy needed to maintain your possessions may spread you thin and block your enjoyment of them.

Letting your material possessions dictate the course of your life is what is called the "trap of materialism." Do not become so attached to material things that you give up your freedom to enjoy life by becoming a slave to their maintenance. If you are working day and night to pay the price for your possessions and do the things they require, you have fallen into the trap of materialism and are wasting valuable energy that could be used to acquire things that are more important than possessions.

Life's most important possession is also found on the path of self-improvement. If the work of self-improvement is to be a true benefit to you, it must provide something in return that cannot be taken away like a car or a boat. But unlike material things, the most important possession of all should provide a priceless gift, a gift that no amount of money can buy. It should provide a lasting value that adds to your sense of having achieved a successful life. The reward for character development must provide the energy to lead a truly wonderful life and not detract from it in any way. So, you should be happy to learn that the ultimate benefit of self-improvement really is something priceless, something of incalculable value that is sought after by every human being on the planet every instant of their life whether they know it or not.

CHAPTER THIRTY-FIVE

Peace of Mind

*I*f you stop and think about it, in the final examination of life there is only one possession that truly matters, peace of mind. Peace of mind cannot be bought or sold; no one can give it to you or take it away. It belongs to you by virtue of your actions and the thoughts you hold in your subconscious. Every action you take, whether you realize it or not, attempts, no matter how imperfectly, to take you on the path you think will lead to peace of mind. Peace of mind comes from a deep sense of knowing who you are, what you are supposed to do with your life and having the courage to be that person. Being yourself is easiest if your actions reflect the best that you can be. Peace of mind is, therefore, easiest to attain when you are in the process of doing something worthwhile, something you think is important.

People often mistakenly believe that having wealth and fame will provide them with peace of mind. But nothing could be further from the truth. While it is true that having wealth and fame does not prohibit a person from attaining peace of mind it does not guarantee it either. Peace of mind comes from a higher plane of knowledge that does not involve wealth or fame

To achieve peace of mind, people must realize they are worthwhile as they are and that they are necessary to the proper functioning of the universe. Peace of mind comes from the realization they are in control of all aspects of their life. Peace of mind comes from a feeling that they are strong, healthy, intelligent and entitled to participate freely in the working of the universe at any level. In essence, peace of mind allows them to exist in a state of inner peace regardless of their physical surroundings. It is the worthiest goal of all and cannot be directly attained, since it is the result of a way of life.

Those who have attained peace of mind stand out in a crowd. The fact that they have attained peace of mind shows on their faces and is reflected in their actions. They are kind and respectful to all people regardless of rank or social standing. Yet, they are not doormats or pushovers that give way to all others. They have a relaxed air about them, a sense of humor and are, therefore, pleasant to be with. They possess a firm, but unobtrusive, dedication to self-improvement and the achievement of their goals. They may or may not have material possessions but they do have the influence of possessions in perspective. The people on the path of peace of mind do not strive for it. Instead they are, in every instance, the best person he or she can be. They know if they approach their life in this way, peace of mind will come to them as easily as the warmth of the sun.

The path to peace of mind can be tricky because it requires a sense of inner balance. This sense of inner balance encompasses two elements: a sense of self-worth and a sense of integrity. A sense of self-worth requires personal acceptance of the fact that you are a valuable part of the universe and not here by accident. Your sense of self-worth will increase as you begin to direct your life to the achievement of worthwhile goals. Remember, only you and your assistants determine the worthiness of a goal. Never take another person's goal to be your own unless you know for certain that it is also right for you. Your sense of self worth will increase when you see yourself as having a unique mixture of talents that are essential to the functioning of the universe. Until you truly know yourself and feel comfortable with the sense of entitlement provided by a life lived in accordance with the universal laws, your peace of mind will remain elusive. Your importance in the universe is already a fact but you must do the work within yourself to realize it.

CHAPTER THIRTY-SIX

Balance and Integrity

*T*he attainment of peace of mind arises, in part, from the feelings of balance and integrity. The feeling of being in balance arises from our sense of being at one with the universe. Our sense of integrity arises from our sense of being at one with ourselves. Both feelings are developed by use of the creative process.

Balance: Balance is a hard-to-describe feeling that imparts to you a sense that you are part of the universe and in tune with its ebb and flow. It is a feeling that involves confidence, a sense of purpose and a feeling of knowing that you are doing the right thing. Buddhists refer to doing the right thing as the Eight-Fold Path. The following are the eight aspects of the path: right views, right intent, right speech, right conduct, right livelihood, right effort, right mindfulness and right concentration. Buddhists are human beings, and like all human beings, filled with distractions and temptations just like you. Being a Buddhist striving to walk the eight-fold path to "enlightenment" isn't easy. But knowing the elements they think will lead to peace of mind and seeking to be on the path, however imperfectly, will help you in your approach the idea of attaining balance and peace of mind.

You cannot directly strive to develop a sense of balance or walk the eight-fold path to peace of mind. You can't say today I'm going to be balanced, or today I'm going to experience peace of mind. These feelings arise naturally from inside. They are the result of an expanded awareness attained through living a life in tune with universal law and working to attain your personal goals.

I cannot honestly say after 25 years of work I have yet achieved an on going feeling of peace of mind or a sense of balance in all areas. But over the years I have made choices and achieved goals that are compatible with my own self-assessment. As a middle school teacher, I feel I have chosen a worthy livelihood. I continue to work on self-worth and integrity, but perfection in these areas is a long way off for me. However, I do feel my appreciation for the natural wonders of life has expanded. I stop in the middle of my day and look up in amazement at the beauty of the sky and trees. I am better able to see myself as I really am. As such, I don't consider myself as important as I once did. I strive to realize the implications of Law II on a moment-by-moment basis. I am certain that I am a better person than I was 20 years ago, and I intend to keep up the work of self-improvement until my last day. I do not discuss my journey of self-improvement and my attempts of attaining a sense of self-worth or walking the eight fold path with anyone. Nor is there any point in going around talking about how balanced I intend to become or how much peace of mind I experienced yesterday. These qualities of my life, such as they are, are reflected in my countenance for all to see and talking about them would only diminish them.

Integrity: Integrity is defined as being whole or of sound moral character. Integrity also involves a strong sense of self worth and a feeling that your character and moral foundation are connected within you to form a solid base, a rock if you will, for your actions. Do not mistake a clear sense of self worth and morality with prudishness or abstemiousness.

You can live according to universal law and still be "wild and crazy." It's just that beneath the life-loving exterior must exist a person who has an unshakeable base of moral standards to live by. This brings us to the questions: What are legitimate moral standards and what is good character?

Most of the moral values in which you believe came from the society in which you were raised. They serve as valuable guidelines for existence within a society, especially if they arise from applications of Law II. Within any group of people the question of what is moral varies from person to person, and acceptable moral behavior can vary significantly from society to society.

If we examine the moral behavior of any society, we will find that most of the moral expectations of that society are situational and easily discarded when they get in the way. If you investigate morality you find many of the moral values are actually only expectations other people have about how they think you should behave and, therefore, are not encompassed by Law II. Yet Law II must encompass the essence of all moral behavior if it is to be truly moral.

There is, of course, general agreement on the major moral issues of life in any society. Lying, cheating, stealing, violence, murder and rape are all universally condemned. Even violation of some of these major issues can be overlooked in special incidences—war and self-defense—for instance. So the issue of what is right and wrong in many instances can still be considered situational rather than absolute.

In the lesser issues, situational applications of moral behavior can be even more difficult. Trying to pick your way through the right and wrong of morals and customs can inhibit you to the point where you fail to do the work of your own self-improvement. Sometimes, it can become impossible to consciously know what to do. It is at this point that our inner spirit and sense of integrity comes to save us.

When you act with a sense of integrity you act in accordance with your own inner moral values. What you do on the objective level must be in harmony with the moral values you hold at the subjective level or you will not be acting with integrity. The worthiness of your values depends upon how they work for you.

For example, if you believe that the meek will one day inherit the earth, and then live in an outwardly non-confrontational way (hoping to inherit the earth), you may seethe inside at the injustices done to you. The moral value of meekness may be doing you a disservice as compared to a more confrontational approach because being meek increases your stress level. Therefore, you may want to change your moral values regarding personal interactions and be more assertive.

Changing the value of personal behavior with regard to confrontation may cause some objective level conflicts but the change may ease the inner turmoil you feel when you avoid conflict at all costs. You must decide what is best for you by being aware of your reactions to the situations as they arise. If your nonconfrontational actions cause you to feel stress, it may be best to modify your behavior so as to be more courageous, less meek and to experience less stress and inner turmoil.

The point in behavior modification is not to go from one extreme to the other but to seek a more balanced, less extreme, position that will allow you to feel less stressful and more in tune with your inner self. Do not intellectualize your reactions to stress-causing values. Go into your levels, talk to your assistants and find out how you really feel. Then align your feelings with your moral values or change your moral values to align with your true inner feelings.

CHAPTER THIRTY-SEVEN

Stress and Guilt

*I*f you fail to strike a balance between the values you hold on the inside with the behavior you exhibit on the outside, your sense of integrity sends off several alarms regarding the destructive internal imbalance going on within you. The first alarm is a feeling of stress. The feeling of stress in its most extreme form can cause mental short circuits to occur which disrupt or deactivate the normal process of the mind, even to the point of death.

The destructiveness of stress can be likened to a person tromping on the brake of a car while revving up the engine; vast amounts of energy are being expended, the car is wearing out the engine and brakes, and the car is going nowhere. Stress is the absolute worst and most destructive feeling a human can have!

Unfortunately, however, stress is a part of life and can arise from our reaction to any aspect of life not only our failure to act with integrity. Often times stress caused by everyday life is unavoidable: financial issues, failing relationships or death of a loved one are but a few examples. No matter what the source of stress, it contains the power to destroy your spirit and ruin your enjoyment of, or even put an end to your life.

Never ignore the feelings of stress when they arise. Deal with stress as soon as you experience it. Use your passive scene in nature to calm yourself and then your workshop and assistants to visualize and then change each and every situation that causes you stress as soon as you can. Dealing with and eliminating stress is vitally important to goal achievement and the attainment of peace of mind.

The second alarm you feel when you experience value conflicts is called guilt. If you feel guilty, your actions are, very simply, in conflict with your values. Experiencing guilt means you have an issue you need to resolve. Guilt feelings do not automatically indicate you are a bad person or doing something wrong. Guilt feelings tell you you've got some work to do resolving your objective level actions with your subjective level set of values.

The work you have got to do requires reconciliation between your actions and your values. You must go into your workshop, discuss the guilt causing issue with your assistants and decide what sort of modification to make. Make no mistake: when you feel guilt, either your values or your behavior will need to be modified if you intend to act with integrity. The only question is, what should you do? Should you modify a particular value or modify your actions with regard to that value?

Viewed in this way, guilt is a valuable emotion. Feeling guilty tells you that an opportunity for growth and self-improvement is at hand. As soon as you and your assistants make a decision about the guilt causing issue, your feeling of guilt will stop immediately. If the feeling of guilt persists, then you and your assistants have not resolved the issue and have more work to do.

When you do the work required for true change your feeling of guilt will end. This is so because ending the feeling of guilt is the result of a true change of attitude. The ending of the feeling of guilt is applicable for all situations regarding integrity, not just the minor ones. If, for example, you were a thief who stole a million dollars and felt guilty about stealing, your feeling of guilt would stop the instant you made a firm, subjective decision to stop stealing. You would still have to pay the price for past actions, but you would no longer feel guilty about what you did.

Often the resolution of guilt and stress requires an apology. If you feel the need to apologize to someone, do it as soon as possible. Don't wait. Don't harbor the guilt and the stress that it causes any longer than you have to. Take the person aside in a private space and apologize in a quiet, sincere tone. When you apologize, do not expect a particular reaction from the other person like forgiveness. They still have the right to be upset. You apologize to end the stress caused by your feelings of guilt, not for the other person. Your apology may or may not make the other person feel better. They still have the right to work out the issue in their own time. They may or may not forgive you; they have a right to their feelings too, and you have no right to expect a favorable reaction from them.

Some people feel that apologizing is a sign of weakness or an admission of wrongdoing. Therefore, they will be admitting they are weak and wrong if they apologize. An apology should not be associated with weakness or wrongdoing but rather a stress reducing act and an expression of regret at doing something that is not in tune with your values. The people who won't apologize because they think it implies weakness fail to recognize that the ultimate weakness is the need to always be strong.

CHAPTER THIRTY-EIGHT

Rationalizations

When you act out of tune with your values, you will know it because you will feel guilt or regret. If you fail to make things right even though you feel a sense of regret, it is because you have dreamed up reasons why you shouldn't. These conjured-up reasons for failing to do the right thing are called "rationalizations." Rationalizations are justifications of your guilt-causing actions that you, deep down, don't believe are in tune with your moral values. When you rationalize, you conjure up feelings you would like to think you feel rather than how you truly feel at the subjective level.

For example, if a person steals, they may rationalize the act by saying that the person they stole from was insured or had more than they needed. Thieves never stop to understand that the rationalization of their theft was in response to their violation of their own sense of integrity. A thief's sense of outraged when someone steals from them validates their moral value of not stealing. What the thief fails to realize is that the rationalized act of stealing only suppresses their sense of guilt and does not actually change how they feel. Suppressed guilt cannot be resolved until the thief, in their subconscious, confronts the moral issue of theft. Guilt in the subconscious level will continue to create situations that will, in turn, cause the feeling of guilt. The guilt cycle repeats itself until the person decides to face the issue that causes the guilt and make a change in their actions.

When resolving guilt it is important to realize that a rock-solid set of values is hard to come by and a hasty change in one value may have negative repercussions on other values. Honesty, courtesy and respect are valuable assets in a world full of people. Therefore, values should not be changed for transient reasons. Take care when you address your guilt and never change your values with only superficial consideration of the issue. Make sure that you and your assistants discuss the matter thoroughly and that the change in your moral values is the result of clearly identifiable changes that have taken place within you and not a situational rationalization of your actions.

The point of dealing with guilt is to attain your peace of mind. If you make hasty value changes, your path to peace of mind may be longer as you retrace your steps to undo past mistakes. But peace of mind, no matter how long it takes to experience, is well worth the effort.

CHAPTER THIRTY-NINE

Growth or Maintenance

*I*f you decide to learn the process, from this day forward you will be faced with two issues regarding your power of choice. The issues are the choice to grow or the choice to maintain. How you react to these two options will determine your ability to live a successful life.

Choices for growth involve change: change of attitude, change in relationships, change of occupation, changes of values and all other choices that will support your evolution to becoming a better person. Some changes will come quickly, some will take time, some will require courage, and some will seem easy and fun. If you reflect upon the concept of growth, you will realize that growth is directly related to life. All living things must continue to grow or begin the process of dying. So a choice to grow directly equates to a choice to live. You will never be more alive than when you are going through the process of change required by a decision to grow.

On the other hand, choices for maintenance require a decision to stay where you are in your life: to stick it out, to stubbornly endure, to refuse to change, to give in to your fears and ignore the urge within you to get out of the rut you have created for yourself. When making a choice to maintain you choose to be safe and merely survive rather than seek the thrill of an active, growing life. The choice for maintenance inevitably leads to a life of quiet desperation. Growth or maintenance, the choice is yours.

Two elements of conflict are stirring within you now as a result of reading this book. There is the part of you that desperately wants to begin a life of self-determination. But there is another part of you, the part that is probably in control now, that wants to maintain things the way they are. Your choice, I suspect, will depend in large part upon your perception of your present circumstances.

If you perceive the life you live now as good and satisfying, then you will have little motivation to change. However, be aware that even if you have everything you want, it does not mean that you should not learn to apply the creative process to your life and assist others with your newly acquired skills. You may find that as the future unfolds, you want something new, something other than what you have now. The processes in this book will be the surest way to help you clearly define and achieve your future goals.

The journey of life does not lead to a specific, predetermined destination because as you live more growth or maintenance decisions will be required and those will affect where your ultimate destination lies. Life requires motion as you journey down the path; the scenery is supposed to change as you go along.

The goal of living a successful life should never be finding a safe haven and then staying there at all costs. A successful life should be exciting and interesting and contain challenges and adventure. The creative process has been provided so that you can move, change, and attain peace of mind as you go along. The journey may lead you to exciting and interesting places and a more fulfilling life no matter how satisfying your life is now. Siddhartha Guatama, who became the great Buddha, began his life as the privileged son of a prince in northern India. He gave up all that he had to become a penniless, starving beggar and then evolve to a spiritual leader of monumental impact. Clearly, he walked an exciting path of life guided only by the principles of service to humanity and self-improvement.

However, most people are fearful of new approaches to life. They are still bound by the programs they learned in adolescence. They are afraid of what people might think if they change their lifestyle, make new friends, try new things and live in new places. They see an airliner flying high above or a ship leave port and they wonder where it is going and imagine what adventures might lay ahead for the passengers. They wonder if someday they might be a traveler on the road of life. Then their sense of "reality" sets in and the power of their fears corrals them. Rather than gather their courage and face their fears and make a choice to grow, they snuggle back into the familiar rut of their daily routine. They stop and think only in the objective level because they don't know what else to do. They rationalize their choice for maintenance with objective level logic. Often people, when they are in their last days, look back with regret on the growth opportunities they did not choose.

Stopping and thinking is a good idea if you have a mechanism set up that enables you to make a clear evaluation of the impact your decisions have on your life and the lives of those around you. But the trouble is that, unlike you now, most people don't have a process for making sound, life-changing decisions. They use only objective level logic and fail to take into account how they feel deep down. They make decisions based upon fear of ridicule or fear of what other people will think. They spend their lives seeking approval from others. This causes them to doubt the validity of their own desires; they become off balance and unsure of themselves. The desire to live for the approval of others erodes their confidence because they are never sure what the others really want them to do. Consequently, they live a washed out, unfulfilled version of their life, plagued by self-doubt and indecision. Life is a gift, and the span of our days is so short. What a shame it would be to waste it trying to figure out what others want you to do.

If you have prior commitments it is, of course, necessary to take into account the feelings of the people close to you, especially spouses and children, when making your life's decisions. You might be surprised to find that your assistants can create a way for your family to accompany you on the journey. After all, your family is guided by the same principles that guide you; they might respond to the same desire for growth and adventure as you. Wouldn't it be great if the whole family set off on an entirely new journey together?

Never forget your have a right to your destiny and time is a thief that makes your life shorter each passing day. I would be the last person to advise you to run out on your commitments, you made them and you must keep them. However, as time passes, commitments change and the opportunity to fulfill your destiny will come to you in a way that you can accept if you look for it. Until that day, it will be up to you to be ready to fulfill your destiny and act when that moment comes.

Lingering curiosity or desire usually contains a growth opportunity or a resolution of some area of inner conflict or confusion. If there is something that is always in the back of your mind, check it out. My father once said, "Don't die not knowing." The curiosity you feel, that desire, that burning interest is there for a reason. See what's behind it. If you have a deep desire to end one career and begin another, don't be afraid to go for it. Hold a clear vision of the new direction you want to take. Be sure to include plenty of desire and courage. Your new direction will take shape. Things will work themselves out. They always do.

You have a right to live your life. You alone should determine the quality and direction of your life from what you think you deserve. Why would you settle for part of life when you could have a full, exciting life? The question is simple but a serious and provocative: What do you want? What kind of life do you deserve? Make no mistake that is the ultimate question, and no one can answer it but you.

As you begin your journey, remember to focus on achieving your goals as well as the 3-Rs. Respect all others, take responsibility for yourself and your life, and get results. Accomplish something you believe to be worthwhile. What is the point of learning this invaluable information if not to create a better life? Remember, you now have knowledge of the process of creation. This gives you the means to define and achieve your goals. Use the your new tools and don't let your life slip into a pointless rut.

CHAPTER FORTY

The New Beginning

Now you know there is a goal achievement process that is equally available to all humankind. You have learned the process comes wrapped in a set of laws that are always in force. You know you can be creative and achieve the goals you set for yourself. You understand the rights and responsibilities the use of the process for goal achievement entails. Rest assured there are no other secrets lying deeper in the basement of humanity. You have the knowledge of the wisest human beings who ever lived. There is no secret society that knows more than you do now about the workings of the world.

The processes of which you are now aware can forever alter your life for the better, if you want them to. For reasons known only to you, perhaps without your conscious knowledge, you have sought out the basic secrets of life, and by the power of Law I they have manifested for you. You now have the one thing that most people want, and at the same time fear. You have knowledge of a process that allows you to make a choice, set a goal and make it happen. As a result of this knowledge, you can never again blame your present conditions and circumstances on anyone else. You, by the power of your own thoughts, have made your life what it is today. And if you wish, you can change it.

The changes you make in your life may not happen overnight; you will have to work for what you want. But now you know that if you want it, you will have it. If you practice the process you will achieve your goal and your desires will become real. You have control and can now live out your version of a successful life.

For some people, the fact that humankind has the power of creativity will seem too good to be true. They will not take control of the power of creativity within them because they think the power is too good for them. They don't feel worthy of a gift as wonderful as personal creativity. Thus, they will be trapped in the rut of their life created by their self image and their existing bank of knowledge.

Others will be rooted by the fear of change to their present conditions and circumstances even if they are less than they desire. They'll lack the courage to change because change requires the courage to face the unknown and unfamiliar. The Chinese have a saying that describes this point of view perfectly: "Better the devil you know than the devil you don't know." This means that some people fear change because they fear that they may encounter even worse conditions if they try something new. But I rather doubt it will be true in this case, unless that's what you want. Law I really is the basis for our lives, and I am certain that you can create something better for yourself if you want it.

Now you have a decision to make. You may choose to maintain your present way of life, or you may choose to take a new look at your life using the laws and processes presented here. You can either set this book down or wonder, intellectually, if the information it contains is valid, or you can go back to the beginning, learn the process, put it to the test and find out if it is valid for you. You will not, however, be able to ever forget what you have read. The possibilities contained in the process of which you are now aware will be too enticing to the part of you that wants to be creative and in control of your life. You will either use the creative process or be nagged, in the back of your mind, with the missed opportunity you have chosen; the "couldas and shouldas" that you will regret not having tried.

Think of the information in this book as a treasure map. This map can lead directly to your goals and peace of mind. Following this treasure map requires an adventuresome spirit, the courage and resolve to overcome all obstacles, and the desire to accept change. Most of all, the journey requires a conviction that you have a right to enjoy the rewards you find at the spot on the map marked with an "X" where life's treasure lies.

Will there be wealth and power or will there be wisdom, love, good health and respect? Maybe if you're willing to work hard enough you can have it all. As an old Spanish saying goes, "May you have health, wealth, happiness and the time to enjoy them."

Your life is now your own. The choice of how to live it is yours too. You have been reconnected with your powers of creativity. You now know you have the ability to define and achieve your goals. What will you do? From now on, it's up to you.

Author's Biography

Mr. Tillman was raised on the Pacific Coast in San Diego, California the son of a Georgia farm boy and a Portuguese fisherman's daughter. He is a graduate of San Jose State College. He completed the Navy flight-training program in 1967. He flew helicopters in support of the fleet in Viet Nam conflict and was part of the Apollo Program, Pacific recovery team. In 1993 received his master's degree in history at Rutgers University.

He has eclectic interests that include, golf, fishing, tennis, scuba diving and snow skiing. He has traveled to many parts of the world, including Western Europe, Mexico, Asia and the Caribbean. Currently, he is a middle school science teacher and resides with his wife and son in Charlotte, North Carolina.

Feedback

If you have questions or comments about this book or desire information about seminars that may be forming in your area, feel free to contact the author at pdtill@bellsouth.net.

To order additional copies of this book you can obtain them online at:
    Inkwater Press (www.inkwaterbooks.com)
    Amazon (www.amazon.com)
    Barnes and Noble (www.barnesandnoble.com)
    Borders (www.borders.com)

Your local bookstore can special order this book through Ingram Book Company by providing the following information:
    Title: Living a Successful Life: How to Set and Achieve
              Meaningful Goals
    Author: Paul Davis Tillman
    ISBN: 1-59299-160-2

Printed in the United States
39981LVS00002B/298-399

9 781592 991600